3-MINUTE
PRAYERS
FOR GIRLS

Published by Barbour Books, an imprint of Barbour Publishing, Inc., 1810 Barbour Drive, Uhrichsville, Ohio 44683, www.barbourbooks.com

Our mission is to inspire the world with the life-changing message of the Bible.

Member of the
Evangelical Christian
Publishers Association

Printed in the United States of America.
06426 0319 SP

3-MINUTE PRAYERS

PRAYERS

FOR GIRLS

MARGOT STARBUCK

BARBOUR BOOKS
An Imprint of Barbour Publishing, Inc.

INTRODUCTION

....

Quiet down before GOD, be prayerful before him.
PSALM 37:7 MSG

If you're like a lot of girls, you connect with God at church on Sundays, but you want to find a way to talk to God and listen to God during the week. This book can help you do that. By spending just three quiet minutes face to face with God, you can enjoy God's love for you and be strengthened to be His girl in the world.

- Minute 1: Read and reflect on God's Word.
- Minute 2: Pray, using the provided prayer to jump-start a conversation with God.
- Minute 3: Reflect on a question for further thought.

This isn't the *only* way to grow deeper with God, but what's cool is that each day's prayer helps you learn who God is and discover who God wants you to be. The prayers in this book teach you how to talk to God and how to hear God speaking to you. When you think about it, it's really pretty awesome

that your heavenly Father cares about everything that's on your mind and in your heart. So use this book to start talking to Him today. He's listening.

GOD HEARS AND ANSWERS

"Call to Me, and I will answer you. And I will show you great and wonderful things which you do not know."
JEREMIAH 33:3

God, I know that You've invited me to talk to You and listen to You. But it's not like talking to my mom, because I can't see Your face with my eyes. And it's not like talking to my friend, because I can't hear Your voice with my ears. Father, I thank You that Your Word promises that when I speak to You, You hear me. And I thank You that You even answer my prayers, in Your own way. God, I believe that You hear me right now and that You care for me. Today, when I pray to You, help me to hear Your voice and see Your face. Amen.

Think about it:

Because God promises to hear us and answer us, what do you want to share with Him today?

FORGIVE LIKE GOD FORGIVES

*Try to understand other people. Forgive each
other. If you have something against someone,
forgive him. That is the way the Lord forgave you.*
<small>COLOSSIANS 3:13</small>

I confess that sometimes I hold on to unforgiveness. I cling to the things my mom and dad have
said or done that have hurt me. I keep track of
stuff my siblings or friends do that bug me. I focus on others' sins instead of noticing my own.
But I know that because You have forgiven me,
I'm called to forgive others. Today, help me to notice the unforgiveness I hold in my heart. Help
me to understand others, love them, and forgive
like You forgive. Amen.

Think about it:

*Who are the people in your life who
have sinned against you—family, friends,
teachers, coaches, neighbors, and others—
who God is calling you to forgive today?*

GOD'S WORD STANDS

*All people are like grass. Their greatness is like the
flowers. The grass dries up and the flowers fall off.
But the Word of the Lord will last forever. That Word
is the Good News which was preached to you.*

1 PETER 1:24–25

Sometimes everything around me feels shaky, and I don't know where to turn. At times my parents are distracted or unavailable, and I don't feel like other adults notice me. Sometimes my friends say or do things I know aren't right. I see and hear things on screens and through headphones that are confusing. But because You promise that Your Word is solid and right and true, I know that You will guide me. God, when I feel confused, speak to me through Your scripture. Amen.

Think about it:

*What is the best way for you to be nourished
by God's Word? Are you reading through
a book? Speaking scripture out loud?
Listening to an audio Bible?*

LITTLE WARRIORS HAVE POWER

So David won the fight against the Philistine with a sling and a stone. He hit the Philistine and killed him. There was no sword in David's hand.
1 SAMUEL 17:50

God, sometimes I feel vulnerable like David did when he was a boy. Sometimes I feel small and scared and helpless. But I know that when young David stood before a giant, You helped him! Although he had no sword, he had a little sling and stone. You gave him just what he needed to obey You, to stay safe, and to protect others. God, be my helper too. I believe that today You are my Protector, and You will give me exactly what I need. Amen.

Think about it:

What are the "giants" in your life—the challenges that seem too big for a young girl—and how is God helping you stand strong before them?

SING PRAISE TO GOD

Tell of your joy to each other by singing the Songs of David and church songs. Sing in your heart to the Lord.
EPHESIANS 5:19

God, I offer my heart, my mind, my lips, and my voice to You. Today I will hold You in my heart and my mind. And with my lips and my voice, I will praise You! Instead of speaking unkind words about others, I will sing the songs we sing in church. Instead of holding sinful thoughts in my mind or harboring ugly feelings in my heart, I will meditate on songs in my heart that only You can hear. May You be glorified as I worship You with joy today. Amen.

Think about it:

What are three songs that you love from church whose lyrics you know by heart that you can "sing" to God in your heart today?

DO IT ALL IN LOVE

Everything you do should be done in love.
1 CORINTHIANS 16:14

God, today I want to love like You love. When I relate to my family members, I want to do it in love. When I care for my pets, I want to do it in love. When I speak to others outside my home, I want to do it in love. When I'm hanging out with my friends, I want to do it in love. When I pass people I don't know, I want to do it in love. When I eat and sleep, when I read and play, when I learn and serve, I want to do everything in love. Be my helper today. Show me how to love others the way You love them. Amen.

Think about it:

What will be different about your life today—at home, at school, at church, or in your neighborhood—if you plan to do everything in love?

TEACH ME YOUR WAY

Teach me Your way, O Lord. I will walk in Your truth. May my heart fear Your name. O Lord my God, I will give thanks to You with all my heart. I will bring honor to Your name forever.
PSALM 86:11–12

Father, I am hungry to learn more about who You are and who You've made me to be. And I thank You that I can learn to walk in Your ways through Your scriptures. God, as I read my Bible today, fill me with Your wisdom. Teach me Your ways. And give me the courage and boldness to walk with You. God, I want to be the girl You created me to be. I offer You my heart and commit myself to honor You with my life today. Amen.

Think about it:

Are you hungry to grow in your faith? How can your conversation with God today communicate that you want to honor God with your life?

WE LOVE BECAUSE HE LOVED

We love Him because He loved us first.
1 JOHN 4:19

Sometimes I don't *feel* like loving. I don't feel like putting others before myself. I'd rather seek my own good than that of others. God, forgive me. I know that You have called me to show others Your love, and because I am Your child, that love lives in me. Because You loved me first, I can love others with Your love that's inside me. Today, show me one person who needs to experience Your love. Help me to notice the one who needs to know You today, and equip me to love that person—in my home, at my school, at my church, in my neighborhood—with the love You've given me. Amen.

Think about it:

Who is one person you will encounter today whom you can shower with the love God has given to you?

THE ONE WHO DOES NOT SLEEP

He will not let your feet go out from under you.
He Who watches over you will not sleep. Listen, He
Who watches over Israel will not close his eyes or sleep.
PSALM 121:3–4

Lord, sometimes when I'm alone—in my bed or in my head—I worry. My mind fills with so many thoughts that it's hard to be at peace, and sometimes it's even hard to sleep. I wrestle in my spirit, but I still feel stuck. But Your Word assures me that I can rest because You are on duty! And because You are vigilant as You watch over me, never closing Your eyes, I don't need to be. Father, thank You for this reassurance that because my life is in Your care, I can rest—in You. Amen.

Think about it:

Is there a concern that you want
to release to God today?

MANAGING MY TONGUE

If a person thinks he is religious, but does not keep his tongue from speaking bad things, he is fooling himself. His religion is worth nothing.
JAMES 1:26

God, You have said that my tongue is powerful, and I believe that it is. So today I commit every one of the words I will speak to You. Help me to speak generously of those who are imperfect. Help me to speak kindly to those who aren't easy to love. Help me to speak Your truth boldly to those who need to hear Your voice. Help me speak encouragement to those who are feeling low. Help me speak wisely to those who need Your guidance. Let every word from my lips glorify You today. Amen.

Think about it:

As you think about the rhythm of your day, in what circumstance will it be most difficult to honor God with your words?

REMEMBERING GOD'S GOODNESS

*I did not give up waiting for the Lord. And He turned
to me and heard my cry. He brought me up out
of the hole of danger, out of the mud and clay.
He set my feet on a rock, making my feet sure.*

PSALM 40:1–2

God, I'm stuck, and I need You to be my helper. As
I wait for You to help me, I remember that You have
always been faithful in the past. You have listened
to every word I have spoken and every prayer I
have prayed. You have protected me and kept me
safe. You've placed my feet on solid ground. Because you've been my helper in the past, I have
confidence that You have got me today.

Think about it:

*When—during the times that you felt stuck
or scared or in danger—has God been the
faithful helper that you needed?*

THE ONE WHO FEEDS ME

"I am the Living Bread that came down from heaven. If anyone eats this Bread, he will live forever. The Bread which I will give is My flesh. I will give this for the life of the world."
JOHN 6:51

God, thank You for taking care of me. You put food in my bowl at breakfast, pack good things for me at lunch, and You offer dinner on my plate in the evening. I thank You that You have given me all that I need. You are a faithful Provider. And just like You feed my body, You have also nourished my spirit. Thank You for giving Your body so that I might live. Strengthen me today so that I can live for You. Amen.

Think about it:

What are the ways that God strengthens you during the day? How does God come to you?

WHAT FRIENDSHIP LOOKS LIKE

A friend loves at all times.
A brother is born to share troubles.
PROVERBS 17:17

Teach me to love the way that You love. Specifically, show me how to be the best friend I can be to my friends today. If my friend is happy, let me share her joy. If my friend is sad, show me how to lighten her sorrow. If she is afraid, help me to comfort her. If she is carrying burdens, teach me how to shoulder those with her. God, help me to show my friends the steadfast faithful love that You have shown to me. Equip me to love like You love, right where I am.

Think about it:

What does it look like this week for you to be a faithful companion to the friends God has given you? How will you show one friend the kind of love that God has given to you?

SAYING YES TO GOD

Then Mary said, "I am willing to be used of the Lord. Let it happen to me as you have said." Then the angel went away from her.
LUKE 1:38

When Mary said yes to You, when she agreed to be a part of Your mission in the world, she wasn't much older than me! But because she loved You, because she trusted You, she said yes. She was willing to be Your servant. God, today I want to be used by You. I want to be a part of whatever plan You have for me today. God, today I say yes. Guide my feet, guide my hands, guide my lips that I might be Your faithful servant in my home, my school, my church, and my world. Amen.

Think about it:

What are some of the ways that God can use you to love and serve others today?

WHAT TO DO WITH MY ANGER

*If you are angry, do not let it become sin. Get over
your anger before the day is finished. Do not
let the devil start working in your life.*
EPHESIANS 4:26–27

God, I know that my anger can be twisted into something sinful. Sometimes when I'm angry, I say things I shouldn't say. Sometimes when I'm angry, I think thoughts I shouldn't think. Sometimes I'll even do things I know are wrong. God, forgive me and help me. I don't want to make room in my heart for the devil to twist my anger into something that hurts You, hurts me, or hurts others. So today I offer my anger to You and leave it at Your feet because I trust You. Thank You for receiving it and setting me free. Amen.

Think about it:

*What are some practical ways that you can let go
of your anger and offer it to God—speaking your
prayer aloud, writing it on paper, telling a friend?*

GOD IS MY STRONG PLACE

My soul is quiet and waits for God alone. He is the One Who saves me. He alone is my rock and the One Who saves me. He is my strong place. I will not be shaken.
PSALM 62:1–2

When I'm in need, I don't need to turn anywhere but toward You, God. I know I can trust You with anything. When I am shaky, I put my trust in You. When I feel anxious about my family or my home, I trust You. When I feel afraid at school or out in the world, I trust You. When I need to be rescued, I trust You. Throughout my life You've been my Safe Place and my Solid Ground. I know that I will not be shaken because You are with me. Amen.

Think about it:

How do you experience God's steadfast solid presence in the midst of your day?

A WORK IN PROGRESS

*I am sure that God Who began the good
work in you will keep on working in you
until the day Jesus Christ comes again.*
PHILIPPIANS 1:6

I know that You are working in me and through
me, God. And even though I'm a work in progress,
I'm confident that You are transforming my heart,
my mind, my body, and my spirit. You're shaping
me into the person You created me to become.
You're whispering Your love to my heart. You're
speaking Your truth to my mind. You're strength-
ening my body as I grow. You're nurturing my love
for You. Lord, I want to keep becoming the girl and
young woman You want me to be. Today, help me
to become someone who knows You and loves
You. Amen.

Think about it:

*What are the ways that God is growing you
emotionally, mentally, physically, and spiritually?*

BEING STILL

Be quiet and know that I am God. I will be honored among the nations. I will be honored in the earth.
PSALM 46:10

God, some days feel more full than I can handle. The busyness of school, homework, chores, church, sports, lessons, clubs, friends, and family can feel like more than I can manage. God, show me how to find my safe, quiet, still place in You. Teach me to be silent before You. Whether I'm on the bus, in the car, walking to school, or hiding out in my room, remind me to turn my heart toward You. As I shut my mouth, close my eyes, and breathe deeply, I invite Your peaceful presence to fill my heart. In the silence, I look for Your face and listen for Your voice. You are my solid place.

Think about it:

Where will you make space in your day to spend a few moments in silence with God?

LIVING THE SERVANT LIFE

Then He put water into a wash pan and began to
wash the feet of His followers. He dried their feet
with the cloth He had put around Himself.
JOHN 13:5

Jesus, when I look at Your life, I see that You humbled Yourself and became a servant to those around You, even stooping to wash the dusty, dirty feet of Your friends. Teach me to love and serve others the way that You did. Show me what it looks like to humbly serve the people who live in my home. Equip me to love the people I go to school with and attend church with. And embolden me to find ways to love those who are strangers to me but not strangers to You. Even when it's dirty, even when it's uncomfortable, make me more like You. Amen.

Think about it:

Who will you encounter today whom
you can humbly serve in Jesus' name?

PRAISING GOD WITH ALL I AM

Praise Him with the sound of a horn.
Praise Him with harps. Praise Him with
timbrels and dancing. Praise Him with strings
and horns. Praise Him with loud sounds. Praise
Him with loud and clear sounds. Let everything
that has breath praise the Lord. Praise the Lord!
PSALM 150:3-6

God, the Psalms make worshipping You sound like a big party: horns, harps, dancing, and loud sounds! Although I don't know how to strum a harp, I do want to worship and praise You with all that I am. I will sing worship songs of praise to You. I will use my creativity—painting, cooking, knitting, or sewing—to worship You. I'll even worship You with my body as I dance, run, swim, and jump! God, You are the One who put breath in my body, and with everything that I have, I worship You. You are worth being praised. Amen.

Think about it:

Can you think of one creative way to praise and
celebrate God that you've never done before?

THE POWER OF LOVE IN ME

*But we have power over all these things
through Jesus Who loves us so much.*
ROMANS 8:37

Father, I know that some of the first believers were persecuted by the government for being followers of Jesus, even being put into prison because of their faith. But during that scary time, Christians never forgot that Your power was bigger than any human power. And just like they believed that there was nothing in the whole world that could separate them from Your love, I believe it too. When my troubles seem big, You are bigger, because there is nothing and no one more powerful than You. So when things are hard for me, I put my trust in Your steadfast love. Amen.

Think about it:

*What is one situation in your life right now
where you need to put your trust in
God's great love for you?*

WHAT GOD HAS PLANNED FOR GOOD

....

But Joseph said to them, "Do not be afraid. Am I in the place of God? You planned to do a bad thing to me. But God planned it for good, to make it happen that many people should be kept alive, as they are today."
GENESIS 50:19–20

God, I don't always understand why some things have happened in my life. I don't understand why I've had to face certain challenges, or why there was a rupture in my family, or why someone died. I don't get it. But, like Joseph, I trust in Your good plan. Even though I can't see Your big design, I trust in Your love. I believe that You can take things that were meant to be bad and transform them. So I offer You the parts of my story that don't make sense and trust in Your goodness. Amen.

Think about it:

What is one thing in your life that seems like a "bad thing" that you can offer to God today?

BEING A CHILD OF GOD

All those who are led by the
Holy Spirit are sons of God.
ROMANS 8:14

Father, I thank You that You have called me Your child. I have been made in Your image, and I am a reflection of who You are. Whatever happens in my life today, I am at peace because I am Yours. And because I belong to You, I want to be guided by Your Holy Spirit. When you lead me—through scripture, through prayer, through Your Holy Spirit, through those who love me—help me to be faithful to follow and obey the sound of Your voice. Let each one of my steps be guided by You. Amen.

Think about it:

As you think about your day, what might be
the opportunities that you will have to be led
by God's Holy Spirit? What are practical
ways that you can say yes to God's leading?

WHEN I'M SAD OR SCARED

The Lord is near to those who have a broken heart.
And He saves those who are broken in spirit.
PSALM 34:18

Lord, I thank You that You know what is in my heart and that You care. When I'm scared, sad, or lonely, You see my heart and You are with me. Today I offer my heart to You. I know that You can see the hurting places and that You care. You notice my fear, sadness, and loneliness. As I close my eyes, I see Your face, I sense Your presence, and I know You are near. God, be my close companion today. Amen.

Think about it:

When you are upset, what is it that reminds you of God's nearness? How can you make room today to pause and notice God's sure, steadfast presence with you?

SAVED BY GRACE

For by His loving-favor you have been saved from the punishment of sin through faith. It is not by anything you have done. It is a gift of God.
EPHESIANS 2:8

God, I thank You for the really good news that You do not hold my sins against me! You know the ways that I have failed to love You. You know the ways I've failed to love my neighbor. You know how I am tempted to put myself before others. And although You know every one of my sins, You have given me the free gift of grace. I thank You that there is nothing I need to do to earn Your love. You pour out Your love on me because *You are good.* Thank You for the good gift of Your grace. Amen.

Think about it:

Is there someone you will encounter today who needs to hear about the free gift of God's love for you and for them?

HOLDING ON TO GOD'S WORD

How can a young man keep his way pure? By living by Your Word. I have looked for You with all my heart. Do not let me turn from Your Law. Your Word have I hid in my heart, that I may not sin against You.

PSALM 119:9–11

God, you know I long to live my life for You. On my own, I struggle to do that. I wander from Your truth. I'm slow to obey. I go my own way. But I thank You that I have the gift of Your Word. In the Bible I discover the truth about who You are and who You've made me to be. God, because I do want to be faithful to You, I have hidden Your Word in my heart. Today I cling to Your truth so that I might live as Your faithful daughter. Amen.

Think about it:

What are some practical ways that you can keep God's Word in front of your eyes, in your ears, and tucked in your heart?

LOVING EACH OTHER

*Dear friends, if God loved us that much,
then we should love each other.*
1 JOHN 4:11

Lord, I want to love others the way that You have loved me. You have been my good Provider, giving me all I need. You have been a Protector, keeping me safe. You have nurtured me, showering me with Your love and affection. And in Jesus, You gave Your own life out of Your love for me. Today show me how I can love my family, my neighbors, my friends, and even my enemies with the kind of self-giving love with which You've loved me. Help me to love the people You've put in my life even more than I love myself. Amen.

Think about it:

*Who is one person you can love today the way
that God has loved you? What is a specific
way you can show that person God's love?*

BEING GOD'S SHEEP

*Know that the Lord is God. It is He Who
made us, and not we ourselves. We are
His people and the sheep of His field.*
PSALM 100:3

Because You have said that I do not belong to myself but that I belong to You, I want You to guide
me today. God, I thank You that I am Yours and
You are mine. You are the One who knit me together in my mother's womb. You made me, and
You care for me. You are my Good Shepherd: You
feed me; You lead me to water; You protect me;
You discipline me. God, because I am a sheep in
Your field, I trust that You are caring for me in
every way today. Thank You for that! Amen.

Think about it:

*What will be different about your day
as you cling to the truth that you are
God's sheep and you belong to God?*

THE WAY, THE TRUTH, THE LIFE

*Jesus said, "I am the Way and the Truth and the Life.
No one can go to the Father except by Me."*
JOHN 14:6

Jesus, I want to know You better and follow You more closely. Because You are the Way, I long to follow You in the sneakers, dress shoes, or flip-flops I'm wearing today. Because You are the Truth, I am listening for Your voice with the ears of my heart and speaking Your truth with my lips. Because You are the Life, I reject false substitutes—entertainment, distractions, worldly pleasures, and anything that keeps me from You—and seek real life in You alone. Jesus, show me the Father's face today. Amen.

Think about it:

*Jesus is the way that we can know the
Father. How will the life and truth of
Jesus point you toward the Father today?*

THEN MY LIGHT WILL RISE

If you give what you have to the hungry, and fill the needs of those who suffer, then your light will rise in the darkness, and your darkness will be like the brightest time of day. The Lord will always lead you. He will meet the needs of your soul in the dry times and give strength to your body.
ISAIAH 58:10–11

God, You know that I long to shine for You in this world, and Your Word reminds me that the way my light shines is by providing for those in need. When I do that—when I feed the hungry and care for those who suffer—Your light rises in the darkness. Father, when I look around me, I see *so many* needs. So I ask You to lead me to one person I can love and serve in Your name. Amen.

Think about it:

Who is someone you already know whom God has called you to love and serve? (If you don't know, ask God!)

WITH OPEN ARMS

*Many people in that town of Samaria believed in
Jesus because of what the woman said about Him.
She said, "He told me everything I ever did."
So the people of Samaria came to Him.*
JOHN 4:39–40

God, sometimes I admit that I don't want to be
found out. I want to hide the parts of myself that
aren't beautiful or faithful. But when You encountered a woman in Samaria, You knew everything
about her—good and bad—and You received her
with love and grace. I thank You that, knowing everything about me, You also receive me with open
arms. God, help me to tell of Your love like she
did. Equip me to share the good news of Your love
so that others will come to know You. Amen.

Think about it:

*Who is one person who needs to hear
that she is loved by Jesus unconditionally,
no matter what she's done?*

HERE I AM, LORD

Then the Lord called Samuel, and Samuel said,
"Here I am." He ran to Eli and said, "Here I am,
for you called me." But Eli said, "I did not call you.
Lie down again." So Samuel went and lay down.
1 SAMUEL 3:4–5

God, the voices around me can be so loud and distracting. I can clearly hear what my parents say to me. I hear the words of my teachers. I hear the voices of my friends. I hear the clanging clamor of the world's messages on television and in the rest of the media. But Your voice is the one I want to hear. God, quiet my heart and still my soul. Help me to recognize Your voice when I lie in my bed, when I wake for the day, and as I'm living my life for You. Speak, Lord, for Your servant is listening. Amen.

Think about it:

What are the ways that you're able
to hear God's voice speaking to you?

HOW TO ACT TOWARD OTHERS

"Do for other people whatever you would like to have them do for you. This is what the Jewish Law and the early preachers said."
MATTHEW 7:12

Father, every day You ask me to love those around me. Sometimes it's easy—when I'm having fun with my friends or enjoying my family—and other times it's difficult—when the other person is hard to love or when I don't know how to love the person well. God, I thank You that You are teaching me how to love. You really make it simple too: do to others what I wish they'd do to me! Lord, I can do that. Today help me to love every person I encounter the way I want to be loved. Amen.

Think about it:

Who is someone you see regularly who is kind of hard to love? What is one way that you can love that person the way you want to be loved?

WAIT ON THE LORD

Do not say, "I will punish wrong-doing."
Wait on the Lord, and He will take care of it.
PROVERBS 20:22

God, I know that Your ways are not my ways. When I am attacked, I want to fight back. When I'm wronged, I want revenge. When people say unkind things about me, I want to respond the same way. But You operate differently than I do. And I know I can trust You. Lord, any wrongs against me that I'm holding in my heart I turn over to You. Instead of letting these fester inside of me, I release them to You. I don't understand Your ways, but I trust You and I know You are good. Today, I choose to wait on You. Amen.

Think about it:

Is there a hurt or offense you're holding in your heart that you can release into God's care today?

WHEN I'M TEMPTED

*When you are tempted to do wrong, do not say,
"God is tempting me." God cannot be tempted.
He will never tempt anyone. A man is tempted
to do wrong when he lets himself be led by
what his bad thoughts tell him to do.*
JAMES 1:13–14

God, I thank You that You know everything that is in my heart and all that is in my mind. You even know the kinds of things that tempt me from Your way. Because I'm human, I wrestle between choosing to do what's right and giving in to the temptation to do what's wrong. But I know that temptation is not from You; it is from the enemy. God, today I give You my heart and my mind. Help me to resist what is sinful and strengthen me to choose what is true, what is good, what is right. Amen.

Think about it:

What is one temptation that you face again and again, and how is God equipping you to resist it?

GET UP AND GO

....

The Word of the Lord came to Jonah the son of Amittai,
saying, "Get up and go to the large city of Nineveh, and
preach against it. For their sin has come up before Me."
JONAH 1:1-2

Lord, when I read the story of Jonah, I recognize
that You invite Your servants to do *big things*. You
asked Jonah to say a hard word to people who
didn't want to hear it. Eventually he obeyed, and
You used him to accomplish Your will. God, I am
available to be used by You. Even when it feels
scary, I want to obey Your call. When I'm nervous,
give me courage. When I'm scared, be my helper.
When I'm weak, give me strength. Help me to be
Your faithful servant. Amen.

Think about it:

Can you think of one time in the
past when God helped you to do
something bold and brave for Him?

I AM MUCH LOVED

··

When all the people were being baptized, Jesus was baptized also. As He prayed, the heaven opened. The Holy Spirit came down on Him in a body like a dove. A voice came from heaven and said, "You are My much-loved Son. I am very happy with You."

LUKE 3:21–22

Father, I thank You that You love me and that You call me Your child. I know—with my eyes and with my ears—what Your love is like, because I can see it and hear it in Jesus' baptism. You sent Your Holy Spirit like a dove down on Jesus, and You have sent Your Holy Spirit down on me. You spoke words of gracious affirmation to Jesus, and You speak them to me. Today I rejoice that I am much loved by You!

Think about it:

How does knowing that you are much loved by God comfort you and inspire you to live for Him today?

AND THERE WAS LIGHT

*In the beginning God made from nothing the heavens
and the earth. The earth was an empty waste and
darkness was over the deep waters. And the Spirit of
God was moving over the top of the waters. Then God
said, "Let there be light," and there was light.*

GENESIS 1:1–3

God, You have made Yourself known as One who
creates light. In the beginning, You created the
heavenly light. When Your people wandered in the
wilderness, You shone at night through a flame.
And Jesus announced that He was the light of the
world. God, I invite You to shine into my heart today. Light up the dark places—where I'm confused,
ashamed, afraid, or sad—and fill every corner with
the light of Your love. Amen.

Think about it:

*Where do you need the glow of
God's light in your life today?*

BEING A YOUNG JESUS FOLLOWER

Tell people that this is what they must do. Let no one show little respect for you because you are young. Show other Christians how to live by your life. They should be able to follow you in the way you talk and in what you do. Show them how to live in faith and in love and in holy living.
1 TIMOTHY 4:11–12

Lord, I thank You that You have always called young people to follow You. Even though not everyone treats children with respect, I am confident that You notice me, You love me, and You value me. God, I want to live a life that honors You. Today I want the words I speak and the actions I take to show others what You are like. Help me to be Your faithful girl in the way I live and love others. Amen.

Think about it:

How can your character show others what God is like?

THE ONE WHO WINS THE BATTLE

*"The Lord your God is with you, a Powerful
One Who wins the battle. He will have much joy
over you. With His love He will give you new life.
He will have joy over you with loud singing."*
ZEPHANIAH 3:17

I rejoice today that I am never alone. You, Lord, are with me in every moment—from the second my eyes open in the morning until the minute they close at night. God, You know the battles I have weathered in the past, the struggles I am facing today, and the ones I will encounter in the future. I trust that every moment of my life is in Your hands. You are the Powerful One who protects me, fights for me, and wins the battle. Through Your power, life wins out over the powers of sin and death! Today I put my trust in Your power. Amen.

Think about it:

*What is the challenge you are facing today
in which you need God to fight for you?*

A NEW FAMILY

*Jesus said, "Who is My mother? And who are My
brothers?" He put out His hand to His followers and
said, "See, these are My mother and My brothers!
Whoever does what My father in heaven wants him
to do is My brother and My sister and My mother."*
MATTHEW 12:48–50

Lord, You know everything about my home life
with my family. You know the ways my family
members love me the way You love me, and You
know the ways they struggle to love me like You
do. I thank You that You have given me others in
my life—teachers, coaches, neighbors, friends, pastors, and others—who have become a new kind of
family to me. I thank You for the ways that these
others who love You and love me show me Your
steadfast faithful love and care. Amen.

Think about it:

*Who is that person who's not in your family—
someone who obeys God—who loves
you the way God loves you?*

EVERLASTING LOVING-KINDNESS

Go into His gates giving thanks and into His holy
place with praise. Give thanks to Him. Honor His
name. For the Lord is good. His loving-kindness
lasts forever. And He is faithful to all people
and to all their children-to-come.

PSALM 100:4–5

God, I know that different people have all kinds of
thoughts about who You are. Some of them know
You, and others do not. I thank You for the confidence I have that You are good! You were faithful to Your people who came before me, You are
faithful to me, and You will be faithful to those
who come after me. Because Your Word assures
me that Your loving-kindness lasts forever, I can
trust in Your goodness, Your love, and Your mercy.
Amen.

Think about it:

In what area of your life today do you need to be
reminded of God's everlasting love and goodness?

I AM GOD'S SHEEP

"I am sending you out like sheep with wolves all around you. Be wise like snakes and gentle like doves."
MATTHEW 10:16

Lord, a lot of times I feel vulnerable, like a helpless sheep. In this world I notice threats to my heart, my mind, my spirit, and my body. In an environment where I feel powerless, You are powerful. Where I am weak, You are strong. I thank You that You are the Good Shepherd who loves me, protects me, feeds me, and cares for me. God, You know I want to be Your person in the world. Teach me to speak and act wisely. Help me to practice kindness and gentleness. Make me like Jesus in the ways I am tough and the ways I am tender. Amen.

Think about it:

Where will you exercise careful clever wisdom today? And how will you practice gentleness and kindness?

NOTICING GOD'S HOLINESS

Seraphim stood above Him, each having six
wings. With two he covered his face, and with two
he covered his feet, and with two he flew. One called
out to another and said, "Holy, holy, holy, is the Lord
of All. The whole earth is full of His shining-greatness."
ISAIAH 6:2–3

God, You are holy, and You are worthy of my praise
and worship. I confess that it's easy for me to get
tangled up in the daily stuff of my life and forget
about You. I get distracted by homework, and
screens, and chores, and friends. But when I pause
to look toward Your face, I see that the whole earth
is filled with Your shining-greatness! You are holy.
Holy. Holy. Help me to stop today to notice how
magnificent You are. Amen.

Think about it:

What picture comes into your mind when
you think about God's shining-greatness?

HAVING A GREAT FULL LIFE

*"The robber comes only to steal and
to kill and to destroy. I came so they
might have life, a great full life."*

JOHN 10:10

Jesus, You assure me that You came so that I might
have a great full life. That is the life that I want!
But I also notice another: the robber who comes
to steal and kill and destroy. The robber who does
not care for me steals what You have freely given
to me. The robber kills the life that You have
birthed. The robber destroys what You have made.
Help me to resist the power of the robber today,
trusting in Your life and Your strength. In You I
have life that really is life! Amen.

Think about it:

*Where in your life does the robber try
to steal, kill, and destroy? How can you
choose for the great full life Jesus offers?*

GOD'S CREATIVE POWER

Praise Him, all His angels! Praise Him, all His army!
Praise Him, sun and moon! Praise Him, all you shining
stars! Praise Him, you highest heavens, and you waters
above the heavens! Let them praise the name of the
Lord! For He spoke and they came into being.
PSALM 148:2–5

God, I am in awe of Your creative power. Your angels sing Your praises, and I sing Your praises. But You *created* the angels, and You created me. The sun and the moon and the stars *shine* their praise to You, but You created the sun and the moon and stars. Even the waters that You spoke into being with only a word splash and roar with Your praise. Out of nothing, You created all that is. I praise You, for You are amazing. Amen.

Think about it:

What is one way that you can
shout your praise to God today?

LEARNING TO SEE CLEARLY

*"Why do you look at the small piece of wood in your
brother's eye, and do not see the big piece of wood
in your own eye? How can you say to your brother,
'Let me take that small piece of wood out of your eye,'
when there is a big piece of wood in your own eye?"*
MATTHEW 7:3–4

Lord, I confess that the eyes of my heart have abrasive splinters that keep me from seeing others clearly. When I judge other people, I sin. It is easier for me to see faults in others—my mom's mistakes, other kids' choices, or a stranger's imperfections—than it is to see the pointy, abrasive splinter in *me* that needs to be removed. God, forgive me. Give me courage to see and correct my own sins, and give me the grace to see others the way You see them. Amen.

Think about it:

*Can you think of one area of sin in your
life that you can ask God to remove?*

SUCH A TIME AS THIS

*"For if you keep quiet at this time, help will come
to the Jews from another place. But you and your
father's house will be destroyed. Who knows if you
have not become queen for such a time as this?"*
ESTHER 4:14

God, I thank You for the story of Esther, a woman
who spoke up boldly for You and for Your people.
Even though it was a risk, she obeyed You. Even
though it was scary, she gathered her courage and
spoke. Even though she might have been punished, she said yes to You. God, give me courage
like that. Strengthen me to obey whatever You ask
of me. In the moment when You most need me to
be a witness to who You are, open my lips and give
me Your words. Amen.

Think about it:

*Has God's Spirit ever prompted
you to speak up when it felt scary?*

A REAL CHRISTIAN FRIEND

These men could not get near Jesus because of so many people. They made a hole in the roof of the house over where Jesus stood. Then they let down the bed with the sick man on it. When Jesus saw their faith, He said to the sick man, "Son, your sins are forgiven."
MARK 2:4–5

God, You teach me and grow me through the powerful stories of people whose lives were touched by Jesus. And when a man in need couldn't reach Him, I thank You that the man's friends lowered him through a roof to get closer! Father, I want to be a friend like that. I want to be the friend who draws others closer to You so that You can touch them and heal them. Today, show me how to love my friends the way these friends loved theirs. Amen.

Think about it:

Who is the friend of yours who most needs to be touched and healed by Jesus' love?

HOLD ON TO WHAT IS GOOD

Be sure your love is true love. Hate what is sinful.
Hold on to whatever is good. Love each other as
Christian brothers. Show respect for each other.
ROMANS 12:9–10

God, I thank You that Your Holy Spirit lives in me and guides me. You teach me what is good, true, right, and lovely. You also help me know what is sinful, untrue, destructive, and ugly. God, help me to cling to what is good and to release what is sinful. Soften my heart so that I might discern what is pleasing to You. Teach me to love the people around me—my siblings, my friends, and the adults in my life—the way that You love. Amen.

Think about it:

Is there something sinful to which you've been
clinging—a thought, a word, an action—that
God is inviting you to release into His care?

KEEP ME HUMBLE

....

Pride comes before being destroyed
and a proud spirit comes before a fall.
PROVERBS 16:18

God, I thank You for all the good gifts You have given to me to be used for Your glory and Your kingdom: my talents, my gifts, my abilities, and my skills. I know that all good gifts come from You. Whatever I might brag or boast about has been given to me from Your generous hand. So keep my heart from pride, Lord. Help me see myself the way You see me. Remind me that all that I have comes from You. Keep me from pride, and protect me from the fall that comes with it! You are the One to be praised, to be celebrated, to be adored, to be worshipped. Amen.

Think about it:

Is there an area of your life where you're
tempted to be prouder than you ought to be?

SIGNS OF LIFE

Jesus said to them, "Go and tell John what you see and hear. The blind are made to see. Those who could not walk are walking. Those who have had bad skin diseases are healed. Those who could not hear are hearing. The dead are raised up to life and the Good News is preached to poor people."
MATTHEW 11:4–5

Just as John the Baptist was curious whether You, Jesus, were "the One," I also have my eyes wide open to notice Your presence in my life and in Your world. I recognize You when people whose bodies were suffering and broken are healed. I notice You when the dead are raised to new life. I know You're at work when good news is preached to poor people. Jesus, I celebrate these signs of Your kingdom and Your presence. Amen.

Think about it:

Where do you see signs of Jesus' presence today?

MY SAFE PLACE

God is our safe place and our strength. He is always our help when we are in trouble. So we will not be afraid, even if the earth is shaken and the mountains fall into the center of the sea, and even if its waters go wild with storm and the mountains shake with its action.
PSALM 46:1-3

God, I'm grateful that You know what's in my heart. When I'm scared or in trouble, You are my protection, my comfort, and my safety. When I'm in danger, You are near. Because You are my good Protector, I do not need to be afraid. No matter what is happening around me, I can stay calm because You are with me. You are my haven, my fort where I feel safe. When I'm scared, I put my trust in You. Amen.

Think about it:

What is a situation when you needed to flee to a safe place with God?

I AM GOD'S CHILD

You should not act like people who are owned by someone. They are always afraid. Instead, the Holy Spirit makes us His sons, and we can call to Him, "My Father." For the Holy Spirit speaks to us and tells our spirit that we are children of God.
ROMANS 8:15–16

Father, I have heard about the horrors of slavery, when some treated others as if they owned them. Where people were always afraid. But that is not how You operate. Instead, You have called me Your daughter. And because I am Yours, I can turn to You as my good Father, Papa, Dad, Daddy. I am not afraid, because You are my good parent. If I ever doubt, Your Spirit in my heart reminds me that I belong to You!

Think about it:

How has God shown you His love and treated you like a good parent would?

USING THE WORDS I SPEAK FOR GOOD

A gentle answer turns away anger,
but a sharp word causes anger.
PROVERBS 15:1

God, Your Word says that the words we speak with our lips are important, and I believe it. I know that the words I speak to others, the ones I speak to myself, and the words I speak to You have power! Help me to be a good steward of that power, using it for good and not for evil. Lord, You know that I long to honor You with my voice. Keep sharp words away from my lips, and inspire me to speak kindly, speak gently, and speak wisely. Today I commit the words I will speak to You. Amen.

Think about it:

As you think about each person you will
encounter today, how do you plan to bless each
one with the words you will speak to them?

EMBRACING A FATHER WHO IS GOOD

"The son got up and went to his father. While he was yet a long way off, his father saw him. The father was full of loving-pity for him. He ran and threw his arms around him and kissed him."

LUKE 15:20

Lord, You have shown me that Your love is like that of a good father. When I have wandered, when I have sinned, when I have strayed, You have waited patiently for me to turn back toward You. When I turn my face toward You, I see You waiting for me, filled with love for me. I see You running down the driveway to welcome me home. I thank You that You show me what a good and perfect father is like. Thank You for Your love that never fails. Amen.

Think about it:

In what ways do you need God to be a loving Father to you?

WORSHIPPING THE ONE TRUE GOD

"Have no gods other than Me. Do not make for yourselves a god to look like anything that is in heaven above or on the earth below or in the waters under the earth. Do not worship them or work for them. For I, the Lord your God, am a jealous God."
EXODUS 20:3–5

God, I know that You want all of my heart to belong to You. And that is what I want too. But I can be tempted to find comfort, satisfaction, and meaning in other things. Whether it's entertainment, or food, or people, I'm tempted to depend on what does not truly satisfy instead of depending on You. God, today I commit myself to be single hearted in my love for You. You are my priority and the love of my life. Amen.

Think about it:

Is there a person whose opinion matters to you more than God's opinion? Is there something else to which you give your time and attention?

LOVING ONE ANOTHER WITH GOD'S LOVE

No person has ever seen God at any time.
If we love each other, God lives in us.
His love is made perfect in us.
1 JOHN 4:12

God, understanding the way Your love flows through me is a big mystery. It's hard to understand. But You promise that when we love one another, You live in us, and Your love is made perfect. God, teach me today to love others with Your love. Help me to put my own wants and wishes aside so that I can love my family, my friends, and the people You put in my path. Show me what that looks like in my life. As I offer myself to You, use me as a channel for Your love. Amen.

Think about it:

What is one way that God's love can
flow through you to others today?

TRUSTING GOD WHEN THINGS ARE HARD

Yes, even if I walk through the valley of the shadow of death, I will not be afraid of anything, because You are with me. You have a walking stick with which to guide and one with which to help. These comfort me.

PSALM 23:4

God, it is easy to trust You when things are going well, but it's harder to trust You when things are difficult. Specifically, it's hard to trust You when I'm scared and when I feel alone. But You promise that even in the dark, You are with me. When the scary power of death is close, You are with me. Thank You for that assurance. When I'm afraid, You guide me and You protect me from harm. I find my comfort in You! Amen.

Think about it:

Is there something that scares you, that makes it feel hard to trust God?

THE BIG LOVE GOD HAS FOR JESUS AND FOR ME

"I have made Your name known to them and will make it known. So then the love You have for Me may be in them and I may be in them."
JOHN 17:26

God, when You say You love me, it's hard to wrap my mind around that *big love*! I know it's true, but it's almost more than I can understand. And Jesus promises that the love You have for *Him* is the same love You have for *me*! That's really big too. He also promises that just as You live in Him, He lives in me. Thank You for this good gift. Because of Your love, I know that I am never alone. Amen.

Think about it:

When you close your eyes and quiet your heart to imagine God living in you, can you picture God's love filling your whole body?

GOD LOVED ME SO MUCH. . .

*"For God so loved the world that He gave His
only Son. Whoever puts his trust in God's Son will
not be lost but will have life that lasts forever."*
JOHN 3:16

Page after page of Your holy Word promises me
that You love me. But I admit that some days it's
hard for me to feel that love in my deep places. I
know it in my head. I even believe it in my heart.
But it's hard to feel it in my bones. But when I remember that You gave Your own life, through Jesus, because You love me, I am convinced. I get it.
I understand. Because You died for me, I know in
the marrow of my bones that Your love for me is
real. Strong. Trustworthy. Amen.

Think about it:

*When you question whether God cares
for you, what are the scriptures that
remind you of God's great love for you?*

TO BE TRULY HAPPY

*Happy is the man who does not walk in
the way sinful men tell him to, or stand in the
path of sinners, or sit with those who laugh
at the truth. But he finds joy in the Law of the
Lord and thinks about His Law day and night.*
PSALM 1:1–2

God, my greatest desire is to know You. Love You.
Serve You. So I want to surround myself with the
kind of people who also want to be made more and
more like You. Thank You for those people You've
put in my life who show me what it looks like to
be Your beloved daughter. And if there are those
in my life who keep me from walking with You,
show me how to gently distance myself from them
for Your glory. Amen.

Think about it:

*Are there any people in your life from
whom you need some distance to be
faithful to God? And who are the ones who
help you to know, love, and serve God?*

RUNNING FOR THE PRIZE

*You know that only one person gets a crown
for being in a race even if many people run.
You must run so you will win the crown.*
1 CORINTHIANS 9:24

God, I know what it looks like for an athlete to run to win. It takes training, perseverance, and determination to be the person who wins the gold. In my mind's eye, I can see the fiercest competitor flying across the finish line either seconds quicker or a millisecond quicker than the second-place racer. God, it's my desire to pour everything I have and everything I am into being the person You made me to be. Amen.

Think about it:

*Is there something God is inviting you
to do in order to run your race well?*

A RADICAL NEW WAY

"You have heard that it has been said, 'An eye for an eye and a tooth for a tooth.' But I tell you, do not fight with the man who wants to fight. Whoever hits you on the right side of the face, turn so he can hit the other side also."
MATTHEW 5:38–39

Lord, Your teachings turn my life upside down and inside out. Your Word challenges me to behave differently than I want to. When someone hurts me, it's my instinct to fight back. To seek revenge. To return an unkind word. That's my natural response. Help me to walk in Your surprising way. When someone offends me, help me to respond with grace, love, and kindness. Fill me with Your love so that Your life lives in me. Amen.

Think about it:

Is there a challenging person or situation in your life right now that requires a grace-filled response from you?

THE ONE GOD SENT

*For to us a Child will be born. To us a Son will be given.
And the rule of the nations will be on His shoulders.
His name will be called Wonderful, Teacher, Powerful
God, Father Who Lives Forever, Prince of Peace.*
ISAIAH 9:6

God, I marvel at Your ways. Long ago You promised, through Isaiah, that You would send a Messiah to deliver Your people. And although we were expecting a mighty warrior king, You surprised us by sending a little baby. And because You came as a babe, arriving with human skin on, living life on earth, You know what my life is like. You know what it's like to be vulnerable, to be weak, to be human. God, I thank You that even though You are the One who reigns forever, You understand what it's like to be human. Amen.

Think about it:

*How was the life of Jesus—God in
human flesh—a lot like yours?*

LIVING WITH OPEN EYES

*As He sat at the table with them, He took the bread
and gave thanks and broke it. Then He gave it to them.
And their eyes were opened and they knew Him.*
LUKE 24:30–31

Lord, I envy Your earliest followers who got to walk with You, talk with You, and eat with You. But there were times when even their eyes were kept from seeing who You were! God, I thank You that back then and also today Your Holy Spirit opens our eyes to see You clearly. God, help me to see You clearly. I thank You for the assurance that You are near. Open the eyes of my heart to recognize You through Your Word, in prayer, and in the circumstances of my life. Amen.

Think about it:

*How do you recognize when Jesus is near you?
What reassures you of His presence with you?*

SINGING WITH JOY BEFORE THE LORD

Let the sea and all that is in it make a loud noise, and the world and all who live in it. Let the rivers clap their hands. Let the mountains sing together for joy before the Lord.
PSALM 98:7–9

God of the universe, You are more than my mind can understand. I know that some people think You are angry. Some people think You accuse. Others think You are absent. But when I see how creation responds to You—with shouts and clapping and singing—I know in my deep places that You are good. You are mighty. You are holy. God, with the seas and the rivers and the mountains, I praise You. I shout and clap and sing Your praises because You are worthy of praise. Amen.

Think about it:

How do you use your voice and body to sing and shout your praises to God?

LOVING EACH OTHER
AS JESUS LOVED US

"I give you a new Law. You are to love each other. You must love each other as I have loved you. If you love each other, all men will know you are My followers."
JOHN 13:34-35

Jesus, I thank You for Your love. And thank You that when I read Your story, I can see the way You loved the people around You. You fed them. You taught them. You challenged them. You surprised them. You washed their feet. Jesus, I hear Your command to Your first disciples to love others the way that You loved them. And I long to do the same. Equip me to love others the way You love, so that everyone might know that I belong to You. Amen.

Think about it:

*How can others see the life of Jesus
in you based on the way that you love?*

I WILL GO WHERE YOU GO

But Ruth said, "Do not beg me to leave you or turn away from following you. I will go where you go. I will live where you live. Your people will be my people. And your God will be my God."
RUTH 1:16

God, I thank You for the faithfulness of Your servant Ruth. When she might easily have gone back to her own home, she committed herself to stay with her mother-in-law, Naomi. In Ruth's faithfulness, I see what it looks like to be faithful and to love well. God, teach me to love others with fierceness like Ruth. Show me what it means to be committed to my family, to my friends, and to all those You have given me to love. Amen.

Think about it:

Who are the people God has called me to love by sticking close to them?

BUILDING ON A STRONG FOUNDATION

"Whoever hears these words of Mine and does not do them, will be like a foolish man who built his house on sand. The rain came down. The water came up. The wind blew and hit the house. The house fell and broke apart."
MATTHEW 7:26-27

Lord, I am committed to building a life that is grounded in You and in Your love. You say that the way to establish a strong foundation is to hear and obey Your words. Today, God, give me ears to hear Your voice. Help me to hear Your Word— through the Bible, through the wise voices of people who love you, and through prayer—and give me the heart and the strength to obey. My life is secure when I obey the sound of Your voice. Amen.

Think about it:

What are the words God has spoken that He is inviting you to obey today?

"YOU WILL KNOW THAT I HAVE DONE IT"

" 'Then, My people, you will know that I am the Lord,
when I have opened your graves and brought you up.
I will put My Spirit within you, and you will come to life.
I will place you in your own land. Then you will know that
I, the Lord, have spoken and have done it,' says the Lord."
 EZEKIEL 37:13–14

God, when Israel was without hope, You worked Your amazing wonders. When Ezekiel spoke words of life over dry bones, You breathed new life into them. I believe that that's what You do today as well. You bring new life to what is dry, lifeless, and hopeless. God, where my heart is dry, lifeless, and without hope, breathe the life-giving wind of Your Spirit into me. And I will testify that You are the One who has done it! Amen.

Think about it:

Are there places in your life that
need God's life-giving breath?

LETTING THE HOLY SPIRIT LEAD ME

I say this to you: Let the Holy Spirit lead you in each step. Then you will not please your sinful old selves.
GALATIANS 5:16

Father, thank You for sending Your Holy Spirit into the world and into my heart to be my guide. And thank You for the assurance that Your Spirit will lead me in every step I take this day and this week. When I look down and notice my feet today, I will breathe a prayer for You to lead me. Guide my steps as I travel, learn, play, move, serve, and worship. When I walk in Your way, You protect me from making sinful choices. I praise You for being my gracious guide and my good Protector. Amen.

Think about it:

How might today look different as you choose to let God lead your steps?

I AM THIRSTY FOR GOD

*As the deer desires rivers of water, so my soul
desires You, O God. My soul is thirsty for God,
for the living God. When will I come and meet with
God? My tears have been my food day and night,
while men say to me all day long, "Where is your God?"*
PSALM 42:1-3

God, my insides are hungry for what truly satisfies. The world tells me that I can meet my need, can fill that hunger, with what doesn't last: food, fun, shopping, entertainment, and busyness. But after the short fix wears off, I'm still hungry. Only You can truly satisfy my dry, thirsty places. So today I set my sights on You. I turn the eyes and ears of my heart toward You. You are the Living Water that satisfies my soul. Amen.

Think about it:

*How does God water your parched, thirsty places?
Through music? Scripture? Prayer? Other?*

A TEENY TINY
MUSTARD SEED OF FAITH

*"Why were we not able to put the demon out?" Jesus
said to them, "Because you have so little faith. For sure,
I tell you, if you have faith as a mustard seed, you will
say to this mountain, 'Move from here to over there,'
and it would move over. You will be able to do anything."*
MATTHEW 17:19–20

Lord, I thank You that Your ways are not the world's
ways. Although the world values what is big, what
is strong, and what is powerful, You have chosen to use what is small. You came as a helpless
baby. You value and honor children. And You promise that when we trust in You, we need just a little faith to accomplish Your will. God, today give
me faith the size of a teeny mustard seed so that I
might do Your will. Amen.

Think about it:

*In what situation have you needed to depend
on your faith to accomplish God's will?*

THE POWER OF LOVE OVER SIN

Hate starts fights, but love covers all sins.
PROVERBS 10:12

God, today I offer myself to You moment by moment. As I move through my day, You know who I will meet. You already know the person who is easy for me to love. You know the person who can get under my skin a little bit. And You know the person who is really, *really* hard for me to love. You know that one who I'm tempted to hate. But You promise that there is power in love, even power to cover sins—mine and others'! I want to love like You love. So when it's really hard, help me to love those who are difficult to love. Amen.

Think about it:

Is there someone in the past who was difficult to love whom God has helped you to love? Is there someone you need help to love today?

OUTSMARTING THE DEVIL

*So give yourselves to God. Stand against the devil
and he will run away from you. Come close
to God and He will come close to you.*
JAMES 4:7–8

Lord, I am Yours. As I move through this day, I
open my eyes to notice where You are and where
the enemy is. When I see the devil—the one who
steals, kills, and destroys—I don't need to be afraid
because I can stand firm in You. And when I stand
with You, the devil runs from me. So as I turn toward You, step toward You, and snuggle into Your
loving embrace, I have the confidence that You
hold me. You protect me. You love me. Amen.

Think about it:

*What are the steps you can take to move
closer to God today? Is there a practical choice
you can make in order to be nearer to God?*

LIVING AS GOD'S LIGHT

Be wise in the way you live around those who are not Christians. Make good use of your time. Speak with them in such a way they will want to listen to you. Do not let your talk sound foolish. Know how to give the right answer to anyone.
COLOSSIANS 4:5-6

Lord, You have called Your people to shine as Your light in the world. And I want to shine for You. God, teach me to live well, especially around those who don't yet know You. Teach me to be wise around people who aren't Christians. Show me how to use my time well. And give me words that honor You and draw others into Your family. I thank You that I don't have to have all the right answers, but that You will help me share Your good news with others. Amen.

Think about it:

Can you think of someone who—with her life, her actions, her speech—has drawn you closer to God?

GOD'S NEARNESS DAY AND NIGHT

*The Lord will send His loving-kindness in
the day. And His song will be with me in the
night, a prayer to the God of my life.*

PSALM 42:8

God, You are the One I turn to when I'm in need.
When I'm lonely, I need You to be near. When I'm
scared, I need Your peace. When I'm discouraged,
I need Your encouragement. When I'm sad, I need
Your comfort. Thank You for being the One who
is always with me. In the day, You shower me with
Your love. And when I lie in my bed at night, the
sound of Your voice soothes me. God, when everything else feels shaky, I thank You that I can always depend on You to be with me. Amen.

Think about it:

*When you're undone, how does God show
you His loving presence in tangible ways?*

REASONS WE DON'T ALWAYS UNDERSTAND

Jesus answered, "The sin of this man or the sin of his parents did not make him to be born blind. He was born blind so the work of God would be seen in him."
JOHN 9:3

When bad things happen, we want to know *why*. We search for reasons to explain what we don't understand. And when a man was born blind, his neighbors wondered whether it had happened because he had sinned or because his parents had. Jesus surprised everyone when He said, *"Neither one!"* Jesus knew that this man had suffered so that the work of God could be seen in his life. And when he was healed, everyone could see—just like he could see—how good God was. Lord, help me to see Your good plan in my life. Amen.

Think about it:

Can you think of a time when something that seemed bad ended up having a surprisingly good ending?

LOVING GOD WITH ALL WE ARE

"Hear, O Israel! The Lord our God is one Lord! And you must love the Lord your God with all your heart and with all your soul and with all your strength. Keep these words in your heart that I am telling you today."
DEUTERONOMY 6:4–6

God, I thank You that You have made me a part of Your family. And when I listen to the words You spoke to Your ancient people, I hear You speaking to me. Today, You invite me to love You with all that I am. God, help me to love You with my whole heart. Show me how to love You with all my soul. And empower me to love You with all my strength. I offer all of myself to You today. Amen.

Think about it:

Can you think of one way that you can love God with your heart, soul, and strength today?

THE FRUIT OF GOD'S SPIRIT

But the fruit that comes from having the Holy Spirit in our lives is: love, joy, peace, not giving up, being kind, being good, having faith.
GALATIANS 5:22

Lord, I see the fruit of Your character in the people I know who love and serve You. In their lives I see love, joy, peace, patience, kindness, goodness, and faith. I want my life to be a reflection of Your character. Today, help me to bear the kind of fruit that comes from having Your Holy Spirit live in my heart. Help me to bear fruit so that You are glorified and others can taste Your goodness. May those who are hungry feed on the fruit that You provide. Amen.

Think about it:

Which fruit of the Spirit comes most naturally to you? Which ones do you need to ask God for help to produce?

GOD HEARD AND GOD CARED

Now after a long time, the king of Egypt died. The people of Israel were sad in their spirit because of being servants. They cried for help. And because of their hard work their cry went up to God. God heard their crying and remembered His agreement with Abraham, Isaac and Jacob.
EXODUS 2:23–24

The biggest thing You did for the people of Israel in the Old Testament was to set them free from slavery in Egypt. Your people, suffering in slavery, were brokenhearted. But You did not forget them. You heard their cries. You remembered the promise You'd made to their ancestors. And You delivered them from their suffering. That gracious movement is how You care for me today. You hear my cry. You honor Your promises. You help me. Thank You for Your faithfulness to Your first people and to me. Amen.

Think about it:

What is one time when you were desperate for God's help, and God heard your prayers and rescued you?

WHAT BRINGS LASTING HAPPINESS

"Those who show loving-kindness are happy, because they will have loving-kindness shown to them."
MATTHEW 5:7

The world says that if we follow its rules, we can be happy. We're promised that we can be happy if we own the right devices. We can be happy if we wear the right clothes. We can be happy if our face, hair, and body look a certain way. Our culture even assures us we can be happy if we eat the right fast food and drink the right soda! But You map out a different way, Lord. Your surprising upside-down way convinces me that I will be most satisfied when I show loving-kindness to others. Show me, this day, Father, how I can love others in Your name. Amen.

Think about it:

Who is one person you'll encounter today whom you can shower with God's love and kindness?

FINDING YOUR OWN WAY
TO TALK TO GOD

"Sing to Him. Sing praises to Him. Tell of all His great works. Have joy in His holy name. Let the heart of those who look to the Lord be glad."
1 CHRONICLES 16:9–10

Different people have different ways of talking to You, Lord. Some people pray in whispers. Other people read prayers from scripture out loud. Some speak to You silently in their hearts. Others sing their praises whether alongside music or a cappella. And some people even write their conversations with You in a journal. Lord, I'm so grateful that You hear my voice however I use it, whether I whisper, read, speak, sing, or write. I trumpet my praise of You and thank You that You listen to me. Amen.

Think about it:

What have you found to be the best way for you to converse with God?

EVERY ONE OF US HAS SINNED

For all men have sinned and have missed
the shining-greatness of God.
ROMANS 3:23

God, I confess that at times I am tempted to believe I'm a bit better than other sinners. When I'm honest, it's easy for me to believe that the sins others commit are a little worse than mine. Forgive me. Your Word is clear that no one is perfect. Every one of us misses the mark—either by a little bit or a lot. But it's all the same to You! All of us have sinned, and all of us need to be forgiven and redeemed by Jesus. Today, help me to see myself as I really am. And help me to point others to the grace You so freely offer. Amen.

Think about it:

What might change in your heart if you
choose to agree with God that all of us
are sinners and all miss the mark?

WHAT REAL LOVE LOOKS LIKE

*God has shown His love to us by sending
His only Son into the world. God did this
so we might have life through Christ.*

1 JOHN 4:9

Father, I read in Your Word that You love me. I know it in my head, and I believe it in my heart. And the reason I know in my deep places that You love me is because You sent Your Son into the world so that I could have life through Him. Jesus gave up His heavenly privileges in order to come to earth and know what my life is like. And because of His death and resurrection, He opened the way for me to have new life in Him. God, I thank You for Your extravagant love. Amen.

Think about it:

*Are there people in your life who have shown you
their love by a sacrifice they've made for you?*

WHY I DON'T HAVE TO BE AFRAID

*"Do not fear, for I am with you. Do not be afraid,
for I am your God. I will give you strength, and for
sure I will help you. Yes, I will hold you up with
My right hand that is right and good."*
ISAIAH 41:10

God, there are lots of things that make me feel scared. I know what they are; You know what they are. When I'm scared, I feel like I'm all alone, but You reassure me that I don't have to be afraid. You remind me that I'm not alone. When I'm weak, when I'm weary, when I'm scared, You are with me! I no longer need to be afraid, because You are by my side, upholding me and protecting me with Your mighty hand. Thank You for Your steadfast love that never fails. Amen.

Think about it:

*What in your life makes you feel the most
scared right now? How can you cling to
this promise that God is with you?*

HOW GOD MAKES PEOPLE FREE

He said to the Jews who believed, "If you keep and obey My Word, then you are My followers for sure. You will know the truth and the truth will make you free."
JOHN 8:31–32

Gracious God, I thank You that I've been given the opportunity to meet You. Through Jesus, I've known You and been known by You. And because I'm Yours, I obey You by keeping and obeying Your Word. God, left to my own devices, I get tangled up in confusion and lies. But I am convinced that Your truth sets me free and sets others free. So speak Your truth to the ears of my heart. Speak, Lord, because Your servant is listening. Amen.

Think about it:

It's easy to get tangled up in confusion and lies, but God's truth sets you free. How will you choose God's truth today?

THE SECRET TO PERFECT PEACE

"You will keep the man in perfect peace whose mind is kept on You, because he trusts in You. Trust in the Lord forever. For the Lord God is a Rock that lasts forever."
ISAIAH 26:3–4

Lord, I confess that when my mind gets away from me, I feel lost and untethered. I worry about school. I'm concerned about friends. I'm stressed around my family. I want my life to be other than it is. I am hungry for Your peace that passes understanding, and You promise to bring perfect peace to the one who trusts in You. Lord, that's me! Because You're a sturdy, steadfast Rock, I do find peace in the storm when I turn to You. Because I can get distracted, help me this day to set my mind on You. Amen.

Think about it:

What is most helpful to you when you need to keep your mind on the Lord? Silence? Journaling? Praying?

MY TRUEST IDENTITY

These children of God were not born of blood and of flesh and of man's desires, but they were born of God. Christ became human flesh and lived among us. We saw His shining-greatness. This greatness is given only to a much-loved Son from His Father. He was full of loving-favor and truth.

JOHN 1:13–14

God, when I read books and watch movies about superheroes, I notice that they can have two identities. I feel that way sometimes too, not yet sure exactly who I am. But I'm confident that what is *most* true about who I am is that I belong to You. It is even more relevant than the DNA I got from my mom and dad. Because I belong to You, I've been identified as Your child. I am Yours, and You are mine. Amen.

Think about it:

Today, share your story of becoming God's child with someone you love.

THE GIFT OF A GODLY FRIEND

When David had finished speaking to Saul, the soul of Jonathan became one with the soul of David. Jonathan loved him as himself. Saul took David that day, and would not let him return to his father's house. Then Jonathan made an agreement with David, because he loved him as himself.
1 SAMUEL 18:1–3

Lord, I know that having friends who are people of faith is a gift. And I believe that asking for those friends is a prayer that You love to answer! Thank You for the friends I do have who love me and love You. I welcome any other friends You would send who can encourage and support me in my walk with You. Show me how to love them—faithfully and consistently—like You love them. Amen.

Think about it:

Who is one friend in your life who shares your love for God?

TRUSTING WHAT WE CANNOT SEE

We know that God makes all things work
together for the good of those who love Him
and are chosen to be a part of His plan.
ROMANS 8:28

God, I admit that Your thoughts are different than my thoughts, and Your ways are different than my ways. When I look around—at my life, at my family, at Your world—I don't always understand why things happen the way they do. Often, it seems like even those who love You have to struggle. But even though I don't understand, I continue to put my trust in You. God, I pray that Your plan, which might make no sense to me, can work out for my good and the good of others who love You. Amen.

Think about it:

Has there ever been a time when
you didn't understand God's plan,
but it ended up working out for good?

BEING SENT OUT BY GOD

"The Spirit of the Lord is on Me. He has put His hand on Me to preach the Good News to poor people. He has sent Me to heal those with a sad heart. He has sent Me to tell those who are being held that they can go free. He has sent Me to make the blind to see and to free those who are held because of trouble."

LUKE 4:18

Father, Jesus was sent out to do all You'd given Him to do in the world. And when I hear Jesus' public announcement of His ministry, my heart longs to join Him in this mission. So send Your Spirit to equip me to share good news with the poor. Teach me what it looks like today to heal the sick and liberate the captives. May Your will be done through me on earth as it is in heaven. Amen.

Think about it:

As you think about your ministry to others, where does it "match" Jesus' announcement about His ministry?

GOD CALLS MY BODY GOOD

*For You made the parts inside me. You put me together
inside my mother. I will give thanks to You, for the
greatness of the way I was made brings fear. Your
works are great and my soul knows it very well.*
PSALM 139:13–14

Father, I hear messages insisting that my body
isn't good enough. A voice nags, badgering me
to believe that I'm too tall or too short, too fat or
too thin, too dark or too light, too much or too
little. But that is not Your voice. Your voice says
that You knit me together, part by part, in my
mother's womb. You made me on purpose! And I
agree that You made my body wonderful! Thank
You for this body that You have called good. Amen.

Think about it:

*If there's something that you don't love about
your body, can you offer it to God and
ask for God's help to appreciate it?*

LIVING LIFE IN THE NAME OF GOD

*The seventy came back full of joy. They said, "Lord,
even the demons obeyed us when we used Your name."*
LUKE 10:17

You sent out seventy followers to fulfill Your mission in the world, and they returned to Jesus bursting at the seams, full of joy. God, I thank You that this is how you operate. You entrust the work of establishing Your kingdom on earth, the way it is in heaven, to people who are a lot like me! God, I long to be useful to You. Send me the way You sent Your earliest disciples. Teach me to act boldly in Your name this day. Equip me with Your power so that I might make You known. Amen.

Think about it:

*What is one thing that God has asked you
to do for His kingdom that you couldn't
have done in your own strength?*

BEING MADE NEW IN CHRIST

*For if a man belongs to Christ, he is a new
person. The old life is gone. New life has begun.*
2 CORINTHIANS 5:17

Lord, scripture assures me that because I belong
to You, I am a new person. The old is gone, and
the new has begun. Father, I confess that on a lot
of days, I don't feel like a new person. I feel like the
one I've always been! It's hard to see new growth
being birthed in my life. But I trust in Your Word.
So I offer myself to You, opening my heart, soul,
mind, and strength to the transformation You
want to do in me. Change my heart. Renew my
soul. Enlighten my mind. Increase my strength. I
ask this in Jesus' name and to Your glory. Amen.

Think about it:

*As you think about your life, is there
an area you can offer to God to be
transformed and made new?*

THIRSTING FOR WHAT SATISFIES

*O God, You are my God. I will look for You with
all my heart and strength. My soul is thirsty for
You. My flesh is weak wanting You in a dry
and tired land where there is no water.*
PSALM 63:1

God, I know that I need You. In so many ways, I
am weak. I am needy. I am hungry. I am thirsty.
I long for You to meet my deep needs and to fill
me with the life that comes from You. Today, I will
look for You with all my heart and strength. God,
fill me with Your living water so that I can be
Your faithful servant. Refresh me so that Your life
can flow in me and through me. Amen.

Think about it:

*Is there a particular need in your life
that makes you feel needy today?
Can you ask God to meet that need?*

WHAT IS IN MY HEART AND ON MY TONGUE

"But I tell you that whoever is angry with his brother will be guilty and have to suffer for his wrong-doing. Whoever says to his brother, 'You have no brains,' will have to stand in front of the court. Whoever says, 'You fool,' will be sent to the fire of hell."

MATTHEW 5:22

Lord, Your Word teaches me that "killing" is about more than stealing someone's physical life. Taking someone's life can be done with my tongue as well. And Jesus taught that diminishing someone by calling that person ugly, unkind names is serious. I understand that it matters to You, Lord, because it shows what's in my heart. What I say and do comes from what's inside me. God, cleanse my heart so that I can bless others with my lips. Amen.

Think about it:

How can you use your words today to give life to someone?

WHEN MY SOUL IS TROUBLED

All day long they say to me, "Where is your God?"
Why are you sad, O my soul? Why have you
become troubled within me? Hope in God,
for I will yet praise Him, my help and my God.
PSALM 42:10–11

God, You have assured me that when I'm upset, I can turn to You. When I'm having trouble with friends, when I'm sick or injured, when I'm struggling in school, when my family has difficulties, You are my good helper. Thank You for your steadfast, reliable presence. When I'm undone, though, it's hard to see You. When my soul is troubled, others wonder why You're not helping me. But I still trust You. Even when I can't see You, I hope in You as my faithful helper. Amen.

Think about it:

Was there a time when it seemed like God wasn't
going to show up for you, but He came through?

IT ALL MATTERS TO JESUS

"Which is easier to say, 'Your sins are forgiven,' or to say, 'Get up and walk?' But this is to show you that the Son of Man has power on earth to forgive sins." He said to the sick man, "Get up! Take your bed and go home."
MATTHEW 9:5–6

When Jesus forgave the sin of a man who couldn't walk, those around Him got upset because He had done what only You can do. They didn't know that it was Your forgiveness, at work through Jesus, that had freed the man from sin. To prove that He was acting on Your behalf, He then healed the man's body! God, thank You for this testimony that You are powerful. And thank You for the reminder that You care about my heart and about my body. Every part of me is in Your loving hands. Amen.

Think about it:

What need would you like God to touch today? Is it physical? Emotional? Spiritual?

A SINGLE-HEARTED PURSUIT OF GOD

If you cry out to know right from wrong, and lift your voice for understanding; if you look for her as silver, and look for her as hidden riches; then you will understand the fear of the Lord, and find what is known of God.

PROVERBS 2:3-5

Lord, I love getting to know You. Your Word and Your people show me what You are like. But I know there is more, and I am passionate about learning more of You. I want to know more of Your mind, more of Your heart, more of Your ways. Teach me right from wrong. Coach me in how to honor You. Show me all there is to know of You. God, You are my greatest desire, more than anything else. Amen.

Think about it:

What are some of the practical ways that you can grow closer to God?

THE KIND OF PRAYER
THAT MAKES GOD HAPPY

"When you pray, go into a room by yourself. After you have shut the door, pray to your Father Who is in secret. Then your Father Who sees in secret will reward you."
MATTHEW 6:6

Jesus said that some people like to pray in public so that other people can see them. But those prayers fall flat. The kind of prayers You love are the secret kind! When I go in my room or closet and shut the door, or when I hide out in my favorite tent or fort, that's the kind of prayer You want, Lord. You've convinced me that You long to be alone with me, having a private conversation. You want to hear everything on my mind and to speak Your Word to me. Father, I'm listening! Amen.

Think about it:

Is there a special place in your house where you can hide away with God?

GOD LEADS ME LIKE A GOOD SHEPHERD

The Lord is my Shepherd. I will have everything I need. He lets me rest in fields of green grass. He leads me beside the quiet waters. He makes me strong again. He leads me in the way of living right with Himself which brings honor to His name.
PSALM 23:1–3

God, when I imagine You as my Shepherd, I can see You caring for me like a mom for a toddler. You put me down for a nap. You fill my sippy cup. You take me to the doctor. You show me how to live. God, thank You for Your tender loving care for me. Because You are so reliable, I can believe that You've got me covered. Today I put my trust in You. Amen.

Think about it:

This week, what are some ways that you noticed God's tender care for you?

SEEING OTHERS' BEHAVIOR
WITH GOD'S EYES

*"You are happy when people act and talk in a bad
way to you and make it very hard for you and tell
bad things and lies about you because you trust in
Me. Be glad and full of joy because your reward will
be much in heaven. They made it very hard for the
early preachers who lived a long time before you."*
MATTHEW 5:11–12

Father, sometimes it feels easy to follow You:
when I'm in worship, when I'm with my Christian
friends, when I'm serving You with joy. But other
times, being Your follower requires sacrifices. It
requires me to give up what I want in order to do
what You want. And sometimes people may even
say bad or untrue things about me. But thank You
for the assurance that I can have peace and joy in
You. Amen.

Think about it:

*Is there a way that you have suffered
because you are a follower of Jesus?
How has God comforted you?*

WHAT OTHERS VALUE
AND WHAT GOD VALUES

His joy is not in the strength of a horse. He does not find joy in the legs of a man. But the Lord favors those who fear Him and those who wait for His loving-kindness.
PSALM 147:10–11

God, I thank You that You don't value me the way others do. The world around me says that what matters most is how I look, what I wear, who I know, how clever I can be, and what I own. But You have other priorities. Your Word assures me that You prize those who fear You. You value those who wait for Your loving-kindness. That's me! That's me! You are my heart's desire, and I wait on You. I hope in You. I trust you. Amen.

Think about it:

Because you know what God treasures in people, how will that change the way that you value people?

WHAT TRULY HELPS ME LIVE

The devil said to Him, "If You are the Son of God, tell
this stone to be made into bread." Jesus said to him,
"It is written, 'Man is not to live by bread alone.'"
LUKE 4:3–4

Lord, when Jesus was tempted, He'd not eaten
for forty days. I know He was hungry! But when
the devil offered Him bread, Jesus refused. He
knew that He was fueled by something more sub-
stantial than grain from the field. Jesus under-
stood that You provide what matters most. God,
feed me with Your Word. Strengthen me with
Your truth. Power me with all that You provide so
that, like Jesus, I can stand up to temptation and
put my trust in You alone. Amen.

Think about it:

What kind of temptations do you expect to
face this week? How can you be nourished
and strengthened by God's Word in
the face of those temptations?

I AM THE LIGHT OF THE WORLD

"You are the light of the world. You cannot hide a city that is on a mountain. Men do not light a lamp and put it under a basket. They put it on a table so it gives light to all in the house."
MATTHEW 5:14–15

Jesus, when You say that Your followers are the light of the world, I know it's a big deal. It means that we are to shine on Your behalf, bearing light to those in the dark. And Your Word reminds me that a small light in the dark—a birthday candle or a flashlight—can light up a room. So I give myself to You today, and I ask that You would use me to show Your light to others. Through my words and actions, show others Your way, Your truth, Your life. Amen.

Think about it:

Can you think of someone who shines with God's light in such a way that it makes you want to draw closer to God?

LEAVING EVERYTHING TO FOLLOW JESUS

Then Jesus said to Simon, "Do not be afraid. From now on you will fish for men." When they came to land with their boats, they left everything and followed Jesus.
LUKE 5:10–11

Jesus, when You met four fishermen at the beach, they were at work doing their jobs: they were fishing. But when You invited them to follow You, You called them from what was ordinary into what was extraordinary, and without hesitating, they followed. Lord, I also long to follow You. Today I offer You the gifts You have already given me, so that I might be used to draw others to You. Give me the heart and the obedience of Your earliest disciples. Equip me and use me to build Your kingdom on earth as it is in heaven. Amen.

Think about it:

When has Jesus called you to do something surprising?

WATCHED OVER BY DAY AND BY NIGHT

The Lord watches over you. The Lord is your safe cover at your right hand. The sun will not hurt you during the day and the moon will not hurt you during the night. The Lord will keep you from all that is sinful. He will watch over your soul.

PSALM 121:5–7

Lord, I thank You for watching over me. Because Your eyes are on me day and night, I know I am safe in Your care. You guard my body, and You guard my soul. Because You have my back, I can welcome each day as an adventure with You. And because You're my good Protector, I can close my eyes at night knowing that You're still watching over me. Yesterday, today, and tomorrow I can rest in Your love. Amen.

Think about it:

Confident that God is watching over you, is there a worry or concern that you can give to God today?

GOD'S SURPRISING WAY

"You have heard that it has been said, 'You must love your neighbor and hate those who hate you.' But I tell you, love those who hate you. (*Respect and give thanks for those who say bad things to you. Do good to those who hate you.) Pray for those who do bad things to you and who make it hard for you."
MATTHEW 5:43–44

Jesus, Your way is different than the regular way people live! Normally, when someone hates me, I want to hate that person back. But Your surprising way insists that I should love those who hate me and who make my life hard. You challenge me to pray for them and even to do good to them! Because I long to follow You, show me how to love the person who makes my life difficult today. Amen.

Think about it:

What one person is a challenge for you to love? What is one creative way that you can love that person today?

I AM PROTECTED BY GOD'S POWER

For Pharaoh's horses and war-wagons and horsemen went in the sea. The Lord brought the waters of the sea upon them. But the people of Israel walked on dry land through the sea.
EXODUS 15:19

God, the more I get to know You, the more I appreciate and respect Your magnificent and powerful ways. When the Hebrew people seemed doomed to die in slavery in Egypt, You delivered them. There was no way they should have escaped, but You made a way by turning the tables on the powerful ones. Egypt's powerful horses and warriors and war chariots were dashed in the sea. But the people of Israel, the people You love, walked through the raging sea on dry ground. Thank You for the surprising ways You protect and deliver Your people. Amen.

Think about it:

Has God ever helped you in a surprising way?

I'M CALLED TO MAKE THINGS RIGHT

"If you take your gift to the altar and remember your brother has something against you, leave your gift on the altar. Go and make right what is wrong between you and him. Then come back and give your gift."
MATTHEW 5:23–24

Lord, You care about me and about the people in my life. Your teaching reminds me that the way I interact with the people around me matters to You. You care about my relationships with family members, friends, and others. When those relationships are broken, You invite me to seek to repair them. God, quicken my heart and open my eyes to any ruptured relationships in my life today. Then give me the courage to make right what is wrong. Amen.

Think about it:

Is there a relationship in your life that is broken or ruptured? How is God calling you to seek healing in it?

HAPPY WHEN I WALK IN GOD'S WAYS

*Happy are all who honor the Lord
with fear, and who walk in His ways.*
PSALM 128:1

Father, everyone around me is looking for happiness. Some act like it can be found by having lots and lots of friends. Some people seek happiness by buying all the latest clothes and gadgets. Others seek happiness by being glued to their phones or other screens. And some even try to make themselves feel better by saying unkind things about others. But I hear You inviting me into a better way. You promise that all who honor You and who do what You ask will be satisfied. Lord, that's the kind of authentic happiness I'm after. Hold me close to Your heart today. Amen.

Think about it:

*Can you think of an adult in your life
who seems genuinely happy because he
or she obeys God and walks in His ways?*

KNOWING AND BELIEVING THE LOVE GOD HAS FOR ME

We have come to know and believe the love God has for us. God is love. If you live in love, you live by the help of God and God lives in you.
1 JOHN 4:16

God, thank You for loving me. When everything else in my life feels shaky, when I don't feel like I've got anything figured out, I can trust in Your great love for me. I learned of Your love in my head, and I've come to believe it in my heart. You *are* love. And today I want to live in that love. Because You live in me, I ask You to be my helper today. Teach me to love others the way that You love them. Let your love touch all those I meet today. Amen.

Think about it:

What are practical ways that God's love can be offered to others through you?

PUT TOGETHER IN MY MOTHER'S WOMB

Now the Word of the Lord came to me saying, "Before I started to put you together in your mother, I knew you. Before you were born, I set you apart as holy. I chose you to speak to the nations for Me."
JEREMIAH 1:4–5

God, thank You that my life was not an accident. I am not here because of any reason other than Your good plan. Just as You knit Jeremiah together in his mother's womb, You also put me together inside my mother. Before I was ever conceived, You knew me. And before I was born, You had a plan for my life. God, I am just beginning to figure out what that plan looks like! I believe that You have a good purpose for me. Show me what I was made for and how I can use my unique gifts to serve You. Amen.

Think about it:

Can you think of someone you know who is living out the purpose for which God made him or her?

LOVING THE UNLIKELY PEOPLE

"If you love those who love you, what reward can you expect from that? Do not even the tax-gatherers do that? If you say hello only to the people you like, are you doing any more than others? The people who do not know God do that much."
MATTHEW 5:46–47

Lord, You know there are people who are easy for me to love, and there are others who are more difficult to love. It isn't hard to love the ones who are easy: the sweet, the pleasant, the agreeable, the kind. But I struggle to love those who aren't as likable. But You have called me to something bigger. You have invited me to do more than those who don't know You, by loving those who are harder to love. Help me, Lord! Amen.

Think about it:

Is there one person in your life who is difficult for you to love? How can you care for that person this week?

I KNOW WHERE MY HELP COMES FROM

I will lift up my eyes to the mountains.
Where will my help come from? My help comes
from the Lord, Who made heaven and earth.
PSALM 121:1-2

God, all around me people turn to human faces to be their helpers. They put their hope in powerful political leaders. They trust in educated people with advanced degrees. They turn to those who are selling products that promise to make their lives better. But I know that my help comes from You! So I will lift my eyes up from my problems and fix them on You. I know that You, the One who made heaven and earth, are the One who will be my helper, no matter what I'm facing. Today I put all my confidence in You. Amen.

Think about it:

Have you ever known anyone who put
more trust in God than in any human being?

THE ONE WHO SATISFIES MY HUNGER AND THIRST

Jesus said to them, "I am the Bread of Life.
He who comes to Me will never be hungry.
He who puts his trust in Me will never be thirsty."
JOHN 6:35

Jesus, You have made Yourself known to me as the Bread of Life, and You promise to meet my deepest needs. Just like my belly gets hungry for food, my heart is hungry for You. And just like my mouth gets thirsty for drink, my soul thirsts for You. I rejoice that You are the One who truly satisfies. You nourish and strengthen my heart, and You water my dry places. Today I reject soothing substitutes that satisfy for only a moment, and I feast on all You offer. Amen.

Think about it:

How does Jesus nourish your deep places
with Himself? What are ways that you
can receive what He offers?

I HAVE A PURPOSE

My bones were not hidden from You when I was made in secret and put together with care in the deep part of the earth. Your eyes saw me before I was put together. And all the days of my life were written in Your book before any of them came to be.
PSALM 139:15–16

God, I thank You that You know me inside and out. While I was still being put together, You knew what every one of my days on earth would hold, and You planned a unique purpose for my life. You knew the ways I would grow to know You and serve You. I offer myself to You today with the confidence that You, who made me, will guide me as I live for You.

Think about it:

Although you may not yet see the big picture for which you were made, do you have a small sense of what God has called you to do and be?

WHAT WE LEARN FROM TROUBLES

*We know that troubles help us learn not to give up.
When we have learned not to give up, it shows we
have stood the test. When we have stood the test,
it gives us hope. Hope never makes us ashamed
because the love of God has come into our hearts
through the Holy Spirit Who was given to us.*
ROMANS 5:3–5

Father, You know that I do not go looking for trouble. Yet when obstacles are in my way, when I face challenges, I believe that I grow from those experiences. Because You are with me, I will not give up. And when I don't give up, I have hope. Today I put my hope in Your love that has filled me through the Holy Spirit. Help me to face trouble today with the confidence that You are victorious. Amen.

Think about it:

*When has God helped you
when you were in trouble?*

WORDS THAT MAKE HEARTS GLAD

Oil and perfume make the heart glad,
so are a man's words sweet to his friend.
PROVERBS 27:9

Lord, Your Word says that death and life are in the power of the tongue, and I believe You. I agree that the words I share with others are powerful. When I speak to my siblings, when I speak to my parents, when I speak to my friends, and when I speak to others, I know that my words can bless or they can harm. God, fill my mouth with words that will make hearts glad. Let me speak life-giving words that build others up. Teach me to hold back any words that are bitter and only share words from my lips that are sweet. Amen.

Think about it:

How can you bless those around you
today by speaking words that gladden
hearts and build others up?

GOD'S TRUTH MAKES ME HOLY

"I do not ask You to take them out of the world. I ask You to keep them from the devil. My followers do not belong to the world just as I do not belong to the world. Make them holy for Yourself by the truth. Your Word is truth."
JOHN 17:15–17

Jesus, I am so grateful that when You were on earth, You prayed for those who were Your disciples. You prayed to Your Father, and mine, asking Him to protect Your followers and to keep them from the devil. Today, that is my prayer too! As someone who is in the world, seeking to obey my Father, I ask to be protected from the devil. God, make me holy and pure. As I spend time in scripture, transform me with the truth of Your Word. Amen.

Think about it:

If God's Word protects you from the devil's schemes, how will you armor yourself through scripture today?

YOU ARE MY SAFE PLACE

Hear my cry, O God. Listen to my prayer. I call to You from the end of the earth when my heart is weak. Lead me to the rock that is higher than I. For You have been a safe place for me, a tower of strength where I am safe from those who fight against me.
PSALM 61:1–3

God, because my heart is weak, I cry out to You. When I feel small, I turn to You because You are big. When I'm afraid, I call Your name because You are my comfort. When I can't see, I look to You because You are light. I need someone who is greater than I am, and You are the strong Rock on whom I depend. You are my Safe Place! Thank You for protecting me from everyone and everything that comes against me. Amen.

Think about it:

When you think about God being your Safe Place, what kind of image do you picture in your mind?

TELLING JESUS WHAT I WANT

Jesus said to him, "What do you want Me to do for you?" The blind man said to Him, "Lord, I want to see!" Jesus said, "Go! Your faith has healed you." At once he could see and he followed Jesus down the road.

MARK 10:51–52

Lord, when You encountered a blind man, You asked him what he wanted. You noticed him, You cared for him, You listened to him. You gave a man who was blind the opportunity to express his faith in You, and You do the same for me. Thank You for noticing my needs. Thank You for listening to my voice. I put all my faith and trust in You because You love me. I love You too. Amen.

Think about it:

If Jesus asked you what you want Him to do for you today, what would you say to Him?

TASTING THAT GOD IS GOOD

*O taste and see that the Lord is good. How happy
is the man who trusts in Him! O fear the Lord,
all you who belong to Him. For those who fear
Him never want for anything. The young lions
suffer want and hunger. But they who look for
the Lord will not be without any good thing.*
PSALM 34:8–10

When I bake something in the kitchen, I don't know if it's good until I taste it. And, God, You gladly welcome me to taste and see that You are good. The proof of Your goodness can be seen in the way You deal with Your people. You are kind. You are merciful. You are just. Hands down, You are *good*. Today I thank You that when I put my trust in You, I don't lack any good thing. You are all I need. Amen.

Think about it:

*What are the good things that
God has given you from His hand?*

TWO LOVES THAT CANNOT BE SEPARATED

*If a person says, "I love God," but hates his brother,
he is a liar. If a person does not love his brother
whom he has seen, how can he love God Whom he
has not seen? We have these words from Him.
If you love God, love your brother also.*

1 JOHN 4:20–21

God, Your Word is clear about how I am to treat my brothers and sisters. Because I love You, You command me to love them. And I welcome the opportunity to express my love for You this day by loving those around me. When I'm at home, when I'm at school, when I'm at play, when I'm at church, when I'm at the store, quicken my heart to love every person I meet. Let my love for You overflow into the lives of these precious ones You also love. Amen.

Think about it:

*What will be different in your life this week as you
take seriously God's command to love people?*

A GREAT LIGHT IN THE DARKNESS

*The people who walk in darkness will see
a great light. The light will shine on those
living in the land of dark shadows.*
ISAIAH 9:2

Lord, when Your people were in desperate need of a deliverer, You promised to send one, and You promised that people in darkness would see a great light. So they waited for the Messiah who would save them. I praise You that when You sent Jesus, You were faithful to honor Your word. From the flickering star above the manger where He lay as a baby, to the fullness of His glory when He walked the earth as the light of the world, Your light has been seen in the person of Jesus. Open my eyes to see the light of Your face today through Your Son, Jesus. Amen.

Think about it:

*How will you share the light
of Jesus with others today?*

WHAT CAUSES JOY IN HEAVEN

*"I tell you, there will be more joy in heaven because
of one sinner who is sorry for his sins and turns
from them, than for ninety-nine people right
with God who do not have sins to be sorry for."*
LUKE 15:7

Father, when Jesus reports what You are like, You seem almost too good to be true. He describes You as an exuberant woman who finally finds the coin she's been searching for. He says You're like a dad who throws his arms around the kid who ran away from home and has returned. And Jesus says that You are like a shepherd who joyfully tells all his friends and neighbors that he *finally* found his lost sheep! God, thank You for these beautiful glimpses of Your heart for the world and Your heart for me. Amen.

Think about it:

*When you look to God's face, do you
recognize the delight He takes in you?*

LEARNING HOW TO ASK

*May He give you the desire of your heart, and make all
your plans go well. We will sing for joy when you win.
In the name of our God we will lift up our flags. May
the Lord give you all the things you ask Him for.*
PSALM 20:4–5

God, You are the giver of all good gifts! You delight in giving good gifts to Your children. God, I
am praying that You will give me the desires of my
heart. And, more importantly, I am praying that
You would make the desires of my heart match the
desires of Your heart: May Your name be known
throughout the earth. May people know You and
worship You. May the needs of all people be met
so that they can flourish. Lord, may Your will be
done on earth as it is in heaven. Amen.

Think about it:

*What is the desire of God's heart for your life
today? For your home? For your community?*

GOD KNOWS WHAT I NEED

*"Look at the birds in the sky. They do not plant seeds.
They do not gather grain. They do not put grain into a
building to keep. Yet your Father in heaven feeds them!
Are you not more important than the birds? Which of
you can make himself a little taller by worrying?"*
MATTHEW 6:26–27

God, Your Word assures me that You care about
the needs of all Your creatures. You clothe the
flowers of the field, and You feed the birds of the
air. And me? You assure me that I matter to You
even more than they do! You know every hair on
my head, and You know exactly what I need. Thank
You for being my good Provider. I trust You to give
me all I need. Amen.

Think about it:

*How has God already met
the needs that you have?*

I TRUST IN YOUR NAME

Some trust in wagons and some in horses. But we will trust in the name of the Lord, our God. They have fallen on their knees. But we rise up and stand straight.
PSALM 20:7–8

When I look around me, I see that everyone needs someone or something in whom they can put their trust. Some people trust in their money. Some people trust in their power. Some people trust in what they own. Others trust in their personalities. Me? I don't depend on anything that's fleeting. No, I trust in Your name. You have proven time and time again that You can be trusted. Money, power, belongings, and charm can all fail, but You are reliable. God, show what it means to trust You today. Amen.

Think about it:

What are you tempted to trust in that's not God? What needs to shift in you for you to trust in God alone?

THE VOICE THAT I KNOW

"When the shepherd walks ahead of them, they follow him because they know his voice. They will not follow someone they do not know because they do not know his voice. They will run away from him."
JOHN 10:4–5

God, when I was little, I learned the sound of my mom's voice, my dad's voice, my grandmother's voice. When I was hungry, when I was tired, or when I was in trouble, I knew I could trust the voice of the caregiver who loved me. And now I am learning the sound of Your voice. I refuse to follow anyone else. I hear Your voice through scripture. I am discovering it through prayer. I hear it in the wise counsel of those who know and love You. Teach me to recognize Your voice today. Amen.

Think about it:

What are the qualities that let you know you are hearing from the Lord? How do you recognize Jesus' voice?

GOD TAKES AWAY MY FEARS

I looked for the Lord, and He answered me.
And He took away all my fears.
PSALM 34:4

God, You know the concerns of my heart. You know what I worry about. You know what I'm confused about. You know what scares me. I thank You that I can release every single one of my cares to You. When I think of my worries like a big, heavy sack of rocks, I know they are too big for me to carry. But they are not too big for You. So, one by one, I take out each and lay it at Your feet. Every concern I have—about school, about my friends, about my family, about myself—I place at Your feet. And as I release my cares to You, I no longer have to carry a heavy burden. Thank You for receiving the concerns of my heart. Amen.

Think about it:

Is there a care or worry that you're carrying today that you can lay at God's feet?

HAVING A BIG VISION FOR GOD'S GOOD PLAN

I pray that your hearts will be able to understand. I pray that you will know about the hope given by God's call. I pray that you will see how great the things are that He has promised to those who belong to Him. I pray that you will know how great His power is for those who have put their trust in Him.
EPHESIANS 1:18–19

Paul's prayer for the first Christians was that they would think big. He wanted them to be able to understand God's big heart for them and for the world. Today I join Paul in praying for Christ's body. Help us to see how great the things are that You've promised to those of us who belong to You. And may Your great power flow through us to the world You love. Amen.

Think about it:

Is your vision for yourself, for God's church, and God's world as big as God's vision?

I AM ENOUGH

Then I said, "O, Lord God! I do not know how to speak. I am only a boy." But the Lord said to me, "Do not say, 'I am only a boy.' You must go everywhere I send you. And you must say whatever I tell you. Do not be afraid of them. For I am with you to take you out of trouble," says the Lord.
JEREMIAH 1:6–8

God, I love that You choose the most unlikely people to do Your work in the world. Lots of folks thought that Jeremiah, David, Timothy, and even Mary were too young to be much good. But they are exactly the ones You chose! You promised You would be with Jeremiah and that You would give him the words to speak. God, I trust You to be with me and to use me for Your glory. Amen.

Think about it:

Has God ever asked you to do something that was bigger than you thought you could handle? How did God help you?

140

NOTHING CAN KEEP ME
FROM GOD'S LOVE

*The Holy Writings say, "Because of belonging to
Jesus, we are in danger of being killed all day long.
We are thought of as sheep that are ready to be
killed." But we have power over all these things
through Jesus Who loves us so much. For I know
that nothing can keep us from the love of God.*
ROMANS 8:36–38

God, when I see big problems around me—war,
violence, people without enough food, people
without homes—I can get overwhelmed. I also
know that Christians around the globe are still being persecuted like they were in the early church.
God, give me the mind of those early Christians
who were not afraid because they knew how much
Jesus loved them.

Think about it:

*Have you ever felt completely
overwhelmed by the problems in the
world? How did God help you through it?*

DO WHAT MY HEAVENLY DAD WOULD DO

Do as God would do. Much-loved children want to do as their fathers do. Live with love as Christ loved you. He gave himself for us, a gift on the altar to God which was as a sweet smell to God.
EPHESIANS 5:1–2

When Paul was lovingly writing to instruct the early church in Ephesus, he was coaching them on how they should live as beloved children. So he wrote that we are to live and love the way that *You* do. And we see what that looks like in the person of Jesus. Father, as I set my eyes on You today, teach me to love the way that Jesus did. Show me what it means to give myself as a gift to others today. Amen.

Think about it:

Are there ways that God is inviting you to give yourself away, like Jesus, for others today?

WHERE I FIND MY LIFE

*This is the word He spoke: God gave us life that
lasts forever, and this life is in His Son. He that
has the Son has life. He that does not have
the Son of God does not have life.*
1 JOHN 5:11–12

God, I am trying to figure out what it means to
have life in You. I know I have the promise of eternal life with You when I die, but I also want to know
what that means for my life today. Here. Now. Your
Word assures me that the answer is found in Jesus. Father, teach my heart what it looks like to
find my life in Jesus. Help me to know Your Son
better today so that I can know You better. Thank
You for the life I have in You. Amen.

Think about it:

*How do you experience or taste a bit of
eternal life today because you know Jesus?*

GIVING THANKS
BECAUSE GOD IS GOOD

Give thanks to the Lord, for He is good, for His loving-kindness lasts forever. Give thanks to the God of gods, for His loving-kindness lasts forever. Give thanks to the Lord of lords, for His loving-kindness lasts forever. Give thanks to Him Who alone does great works, for His loving-kindness lasts forever.
PSALM 136:1–4

Lord, as I listen to the words of the psalmist, I am invited to give You thanks. The rhythm of praise to You is almost like a dance! So I thank You today that Your loving-kindness lasts forever. This is what matters *most* today: more than my worries, more than my friends, more than my homework, more than my activities, and more than *every* other thing in my life. *Your loving-kindness lasts forever.* Amen.

Think about it:

How can you hang on to this single truth today, that God's loving-kindness lasts forever? Send yourself an email? Write it down? Memorize it?

THE MIND OF THE LORD

*God's riches are so great! The things He knows
and His wisdom are so deep! No one can understand
His thoughts. No one can understand His ways.
The Holy Writings say, "Who knows the mind of the
Lord? Who is able to tell Him what to do?"*
ROMANS 11:33–34

God, as I commit myself to knowing You more deeply, I wrestle to understand all of who You are. It's hard to wrap my mind around Your wisdom and Your ways. So today I accept that Your ways are beyond me. And that's okay. Even though I can't comprehend all of Your wisdom, I am able to put my trust in You. In fact, it gives me comfort to know that You are in charge and I am not! Thank You for Your mighty power. Amen.

Think about it:

*Is there something about God or the way
God works that feels like a mystery to you?
Can you give that wondering to Him today?*

TELLING WHAT GOD HAS DONE

O give thanks to the Lord. Call on His name.
Make His works known among the people.
Sing to Him. Sing praises to Him. Tell of all
His great works. Honor His holy name. Let the
heart of those who look to the Lord be glad.
PSALM 105:1–3

God, there was a time when I didn't know about Your great works. I didn't know how You delivered Your people from slavery in Egypt. I didn't know how You freed us all from the power of sin and death through the resurrection of Jesus. And I didn't know how much You love and care, personally, for *me*. But I came to know it all because others made Your works known to me! Today, use me to share Your goodness with others. Amen.

Think about it:

How can you share about your experience
of God's goodness with someone who
needs to hear about it today?

HEARING AND OBEYING THE WORD OF GOD

Obey the Word of God. If you hear only and do not act, you are only fooling yourself.
JAMES 1:22

Father, You warn that if I hear Your Word but don't act on it, I'm fooling myself. And I don't want to be that person! I don't want to be the person who reads Your words, who hears Your voice, and then forgets about You. Rather, I want to be the person who encounters Your Word and then *lives differently* because I am living for You. Send Your Spirit to open my eyes, Lord. Quicken my heart to notice where Your Word intersects with my life, and give me the courage to live in faithful response to You. Amen.

Think about it:

How does your living reflect that you are obeying God's Word? What is one practical way you can respond to God today?

LOVING AND BEING LOVED

This is love! It is not that we loved God but that He loved us. For God sent His Son to pay for our sins with His own blood.
1 JOHN 4:10

Lord, thank You for the reminder in Your Word that before I ever loved You, *You loved me!* That You sent Jesus to rescue me is a good gift that I don't take for granted. And God, let me reflect this in the way I live today. Let me be someone who loves others *first*. Help me to be the kind of person who notices others and loves them without expecting anything in return. Because You sacrificed everything to love me, show me how to love others today with that selfless kind of love. Amen.

Think about it:

Sometimes we love others because they'll love us back. But God's love, in us, isn't like that. How can you love someone else this week without expecting anything from that person?

OBEYING GOD WHEN WE DON'T KNOW WHAT'S NEXT

Because Abraham had faith, he obeyed God when God called him to leave his home. He was to go to another country that God promised to give him. He left his home without knowing where he was going.
HEBREWS 11:8

Abraham's faith in You is like setting off on a journey in a blinding blizzard! He couldn't see where he was going, but he trusted that You had something good in store for him. Lord, give me the kind of faith Abraham had. I want to say yes to You when You ask me to trust You. Believing Your promises, I want to take big risks as I follow You. Give me courage to say yes to the sound of Your voice today. Amen.

Think about it:

What is God asking you to do today that takes some courage? How will you respond in faith?

DOING THE SURPRISING THING THAT GOD ASKS

If the one who hates you is hungry, feed him.
If he is thirsty, give him water. If you do that,
you will be making him more ashamed of
himself, and the Lord will reward you.
PROVERBS 25:21–22

When You ask me to feed the hungry and offer water to the thirsty, I understand what it means to follow You. Because You feed and water Your sheep, I know that I'm called to do the same. But when You ask me to bless the person who hates me? That seems crazy. Lord, I already know that I don't always understand Your ways. And this is one of those ways. Give me Your courage to love the person who doesn't show love to me. Help me to offer the food and water that You've so freely given to me to the one who's hard to love. Amen.

Think about it:

Who is someone who really doesn't like you?
And how can you love that person today?

PRAYING FOR THOSE IN POWER

*First of all, I ask you to pray much for all men
and to give thanks for them. Pray for kings
and all others who are in power over us so we
might live quiet God-like lives in peace.*
1 TIMOTHY 2:1–2

Lord, when I hear the adults around me discussing politics and even arguing about how things should be handled, I feel confused. I confess that I don't know what the answers are! So when I hear Your call to pray for those who are in authority—for presidents, for others serving in elected offices, for police officers, for mayors, for pastors, and for teachers—I want to obey. Today I offer these leaders to You, naming those whose names I know. God, guide them so that all may live lives that honor You in peace. Amen.

Think about it:

*Who are some people in authority, either
local or federal or international, that God
is putting on your heart to pray for?*

HOW I TREAT MY PARENTS

Children, as Christians, obey your parents. This is the right thing to do. Respect your father and mother. This is the first Law given that had a promise. The promise is this: If you respect your father and mother, you will live a long time and your life will be full of many good things.
EPHESIANS 6:1–3

Lord, You've been clear about how I am to behave toward my parents: You want me to love them. You want me to respect them. You want me to obey them. Be my helper as I strive to love, respect, and obey my caregivers today. I know that even though they aren't perfect, I'm still called to be faithful and obedient to You, so guide me as I seek to honor You *and* them. Amen.

Think about it:

What is one way you can show your parents that you love, respect, and obey them?

LEARNING TO PRAY
ABOUT EVERYTHING

Do not worry. Learn to pray about everything.
Give thanks to God as you ask Him for what you
need. The peace of God is much greater than
the human mind can understand. This peace will
keep your hearts and minds through Christ Jesus.
PHILIPPIANS 4:6–7

God, I am learning to trust You with *everything*. I confess that there are parts of my life—that I think about, that I worry about, that I cry about, that I talk about—that I haven't known how to trust You with. Forgive me. Teach me how to take every part of my life and release it to You. Thank You that I can trust You with everything that matters to me. Amen.

Think about it:

Is there something that upsets you that you
haven't ever told God about? Can you speak
or write a prayer about it to God today?

I WILL FEAR THE LORD

Pleasing ways lie and beauty comes to nothing,
but a woman who fears the Lord will be praised.
PROVERBS 31:30

God, I can see that what the world values is not what You value. Loud voices in our culture say that the way I appear to others—my face, my body, my hair, and what I wear—is what makes me worthy. But Your Word convinces me that there is a better way and that what You cherish is other than what the world esteems. You treasure the person who fears You. Because You are holy, because You are above all else, I do fear You, Lord. Kindle in my heart a holy passion, fear, and reverence for You today. Amen.

Think about it:

When you fear the Lord, when you respect and honor God above all else, what are the earthly things that you don't need to worry about?

GOD KNOWS WHAT I NEED

*In the same way, the Holy Spirit helps us where we
are weak. We do not know how to pray or what we
should pray for, but the Holy Spirit prays to God
for us with sounds that cannot be put into words.*

ROMANS 8:26

Lord, when I'm weak—when I feel sad, confused,
angry, or afraid—I don't always know how to pray.
So I thank You that when I have no idea how to
pray, Your Spirit prays for me. When I can't find
the right words to say to You, when I don't even
know what I should be asking for, the Holy Spirit
interprets prayers for me. Even if I just groan, the
right words are delivered to Your ears. Not only
do You hear my prayers, You help me pray them.
Thank You for being my nearby helper. Amen.

Think about it:

*Has there been a situation in your
life when you didn't know what to pray?*

WHAT GREAT LOVE THE FATHER HAS

See what great love the Father has for us that He would call us His children. And that is what we are. For this reason the people of the world do not know who we are because they did not know Him. Dear friends, we are God's children now.
1 JOHN 3:1–2

Lord, I know it is no small thing that You call me Your child. It's a really big deal! On the human plane, I may be a daughter, a sister, a granddaughter, a student, an athlete, a musician, or a friend, but the most important identity in my life is that I am *Your daughter*. And that means I am deeply loved by You. God, today I will soak in the truth that I belong to You, and You are my perfect Father. Amen.

Think about it:

Does knowing that God is your perfect Father change anything about the way you relate to your human father or mother?

THE PLACE OF COMFORT

*Lord, You have been the place of comfort for all
people of all time. Before the mountains were
born, before You gave birth to the earth and
the world, forever and ever, You are God.*
PSALM 90:1-2

God, thank You for being my good comforter.
When I feel anxious, You soothe me. When I'm
afraid, You reassure me. When I'm sad, You encourage me. When I'm weak, You help me. And I
know I'm not alone. God who created everything,
You are mighty. I can read in the Bible how You
have been a strong Rock and gentle comforter
for Your people throughout the ages. And just as
You have protected them, provided for them, and
comforted them, I know You do the same for me.
Today I trust in Your love. Amen.

Think about it:

*Where do you need God's comfort
and support in your life today?*

IF ANYONE IS SUFFERING

Is anyone among you suffering? He should pray.
Is anyone happy? He should sing songs of thanks
to God. Is anyone among you sick? He should send
for the church leaders and they should pray for him.
They should pour oil on him in the name of the Lord.
JAMES 5:13–14

Father, when I am in need and when those in my Christian community are in need, You instruct us to pray. I admit that sometimes I save prayer until I'm really desperate and need You to come through for me in a pinch! But because You love hearing my voice, You invite me to pray in all circumstances. You listen to my prayers when I'm suffering or someone else is suffering. You hear my voice when I'm happy or when I'm rejoicing with a friend. You pay attention when I'm sick or someone else is sick. Lord, I will pray when I'm suffering. I'll pray when I'm happy. I'll pray when I'm sick. I'll pray no matter what I'm thinking or feeling. Thank You! Amen.

Think about it:

Who do you already know whom God has called
you to pray for? (If you don't know, ask God!)

THE WORD THAT
REVEALS MY HEART

*God's Word is living and powerful. It is sharper than
a sword that cuts both ways. It cuts straight into
where the soul and spirit meet and it divides them.
It cuts into the joints and bones. It tells what the
heart is thinking about and what it wants to do.*
HEBREWS 4:12

God, I am convinced that Your scriptures are alive,
and they are powerful. Your Word reveals who You
are: loving, just, merciful. It teaches us how to live
as Your faithful people, and it draws others to You.
But Your Word also reveals what is in my heart!
When I read the Bible, Your words expose what is
in my heart and mind. Even though it's not always
pretty, thank You for the gift of Your Word. Amen.

Think about it:

*Can you think of a passage of scripture
that reveals your heart or pricks your
conscience by exposing what's inside you?*

SWEET WORDS FROM MY LIPS

*Pleasing words are like honey. They are
sweet to the soul and healing to the bones.*
PROVERBS 16:24

God, as I listen to the speech of those around me, I hear different ways of talking. Some mouths spit out words that are unkind to others. Others use words that are ugly or offensive. And some use their words to bless others. They use their mouths to encourage, to inspire, to heal, to bless, and to build up. God, help me to be someone who uses my words wisely. Help me to be careful when I should bite my tongue, and lead me to be generous when I can bless others with the words I speak. Teach me to speak the words You would have me speak. Amen.

Think about it:

*Who in your life consistently speaks
beautiful words that build up other people?*

BEING THOUGHTFUL ABOUT MY THOUGHTS

Keep your minds thinking about things in heaven. Do not think about things on the earth. You are dead to the things of this world. Your new life is now hidden in God through Christ.

COLOSSIANS 3:2–3

Father, sometimes my mind is like a busy playground! My thoughts bounce between things I want to buy, sweets I'd like to eat, people who I think can make me happy, and stuff I want to do. But when I quiet my heart to listen for Your voice, You are faithful to still my soul. You help me keep my mind on what matters most. Lord, help me this day to focus on the things that matter to You. Amen.

Think about it:

What are some of the thoughts in your head that you sense are not from God? And what are the practical ways to redirect your mind to stay on the things of God?

ALL GOOD GIFTS ARE FROM GOD

Whatever is good and perfect comes to us from God. He is the One Who made all light. He does not change. No shadow is made by His turning.
JAMES 1:17

Lord, You are the giver of every good and perfect gift. When I look at all that is good in my life, I know that every gift has come from Your hand. Thank You for the food on my plate and the roof over my head. Thank You for each one of my family members—those who are easy to love and those who are more difficult. Thank You for the opportunity to learn and grow. Thank You for the friends You've placed in my life. Father, You have given me all I need. Amen.

Think about it:

As you think about the ways God has blessed you, what is the most important gift you've received?

LOVING EACH OTHER

Dear friends, let us love each other, because love comes from God. Those who love are God's children and they know God. Those who do not love do not know God because God is love.
1 JOHN 4:7–8

Lord, You have been crystal clear about what it looks like to be in Your family: if we love others, we know You, and we're Your children. Father, thank You that I belong to You. I long to love those around me—friends, family, teachers, neighbors, and even enemies!—with Your love. Show me today how I can love each person I meet. Teach me how to share Your love with those who know You and those who don't yet know You, for Your glory. Amen.

Think about it:

Can you think of an older Christian who consistently loves others? And what will it look like for you to be intentional about loving others today?

WAITING ON THE LORD TO ACT

Do not say, "I will punish wrong-doing."
Wait on the Lord, and He will take care of it.
PROVERBS 20:22

Father, I confess that when people hurt me, I feel like I want to get revenge. When my sibling tattles on me, when a friend ignores me, or when someone at school is mean to me, I want them to feel as bad as I feel. Forgive me. Your Word says that punishing wrongdoing is *not* my job. It is Yours. Lord, teach me what it means to let go of my hurt, my sadness, and my anger. Because I know You love me, I can trust You to take care of it. You are my strong Protector. Amen.

Think about it:

Is there someone who has hurt you against whom you are holding a grudge? Instead of wishing that person harm, how will you release him or her into God's care today?

MY FATHER IN HEAVEN GIVES GOOD GIFTS

"What man among you would give his son a stone if he should ask for bread? Or if he asks for a fish, would he give him a snake? You are bad and you know how to give good things to your children. How much more will your Father in heaven give good things to those who ask Him?"
MATTHEW 7:9–11

God, the Bible says that You are a Father who is good. When my parents put a sandwich in my lunch or fish sticks on my plate, I know that they love me. Your Word says that You love me even *more* than they do! This gives me the confidence to ask You for what I need, and it assures me that You *want* to give me good things when I turn to You. You are my faithful Provider. Amen.

Think about it:

God delights in meeting our needs. What are the good gifts from God's hand that you are enjoying today?

A MAN KNOWN TO BE A SINNER

He said, "Zaccheus, come down at once. I must
stay in your house today." At once he came down
and was glad to have Jesus come to his house.
When the people saw it, they began to complain
among themselves. They said, "He is going to
stay with a man who is known to be a sinner."
LUKE 19:5–7

Father, I admit that being around people whom
others call "sinners" makes me uncomfortable.
Usually I'd rather keep my distance—from kids
at school who goof off, from those in the neighborhood who get into trouble, or even from kids
whose families practice other religions—rather
than spending time with these precious ones. And
yet Jesus moved toward the people His culture
identified as *sinners*. So give me courage to love
like Jesus loves. Amen.

Think about it:

*Is there someone in your life, maybe whom others
do not accept, whom you can befriend today?*

BEING SET FREE FROM THE LAW

The Law was given through Moses, but loving-favor and truth came through Jesus Christ.
JOHN 1:17

Lord, when Jesus came to people who were Jewish and people who *weren't* Jewish, they all had to figure out what it meant to be faithful to You. And Jewish people who came to believe in You wanted to honor the law that had been given by You through Moses. But Your good news means that we have been set free from the rule-following life of the law. Because Jesus has kept the law perfectly and because we never can, He has liberated us from the constraints of the law. Through Jesus we've been given both truth and loving-favor for *free*! Thank You for Your abundant grace. Amen.

Think about it:

*What does it mean for your life today
that Jesus came to set us free from
having to keep the old law?*

BEING CLOTHED WITH GOD'S PROTECTION

Wear a belt of truth around your body. Wear a piece of iron over your chest which is being right with God. Wear shoes on your feet which are the Good News of peace. Most important of all, you need a covering of faith in front of you. This is to put out the fire-arrows of the devil.
EPHESIANS 6:14–16

God, I want to be clothed in Your power, but the clothes and shoes and jewelry I wear don't equip me for the adventure to which You've called me. So today I wrap truth around my middle. I put righteousness over my front. The shoes I wear make me quick to tell others of Your good news. And I'm covered by a shield of faith that protects me from the devil's arrows. God, I thank You that You've given me all I need to be Your person today. Amen.

Think about it:

Which piece of God's holy armor is the one you most need this day?

I DON'T HAVE TO BE STRONG ON MY OWN

*Christ will keep you strong until He comes
again. No blame will be held against you.
God is faithful. He chose you to be joined
together with His Son, Jesus Christ our Lord.*
1 CORINTHIANS 1:8–9

Lord, You know that it's my desire to please You. And yet I know that I can't live a perfectly pleasing life on my own. Thankfully, Your Word assures me that I don't have to! You promise that it is Christ who will keep me strong until He comes again. So instead of trusting in my own good behavior, I will trust in You because You are faithful. And because I'm joined with Jesus, He has taken the blame that was due to me. Thank You for Your great mercy! Amen.

Think about it:

*How does trusting in Christ's faithfulness
make a difference in your life today?*

A PLEA TO BE GENTLE AND KIND

I am being held in prison because of working for the Lord. I ask you from my heart to live and work the way the Lord expected you to live and work. Live and work without pride. Be gentle and kind. Do not be hard on others. Let love keep you from doing that.

EPHESIANS 4:1–2

When early Christians were being persecuted, Paul was put in prison for his faith in Jesus. From his prison cell, he pled with believers to *live well*. Father, I hear that same invitation today: to live and work faithfully and without pride. I also commit myself to loving others by being gentle and kind. Show me, this day, how to live a life that honors You in all that I do. Amen.

Think about it:

As you think about your day, how can you honor God in the way that you live, the way that you work, the way that you love?

HOW GOD IS GROWING ME

And this is my prayer: I pray that your love will grow more and more. I pray that you will have better understanding and be wise in all things. I pray that you will know what is the very best. I pray that you will be true and without blame until the day Christ comes again.

PHILIPPIANS 1:9–10

Lord, as I am growing taller and bigger physically, as I'm learning and growing intellectually, as I'm maturing socially, I also want to be growing spiritually. Help me to grow in my love for others. Help me to increase in wisdom that comes from You. Help me to obey so that I can live faithfully to You. Father, send Your Spirit to help me become all that You've created me to be. Amen.

Think about it:

How have you seen spiritual growth in yourself? What are some of the signs that God is at work in you?

LOOKING FOR GOD

A man cannot please God unless he has faith.
Anyone who comes to God must believe that He is.
That one must also know that God gives what is
promised to the one who keeps on looking for Him.
HEBREWS 11:6

Father, when You make a promise, You keep it. Even though people fall short of keeping our word, You are faithful to do all You have said. I thank You for the promises I have in Your Word. You assure me that as I keep my eyes on You—as I keep seeking Your face—You will give me what You have offered in the scriptures. So today I fix my eyes on You, looking for Your face and listening for Your voice. Show me what You are like, and speak to my heart. Amen.

Think about it:

What is one practical way that you
can keep your eyes on God today?

WHAT IS PURE AND GOOD

*Religion that is pure and good before God the Father
is to help children who have no parents and to care
for women whose husbands have died who have
troubles. Pure religion is also to keep yourself
clean from the sinful things of the world.*

JAMES 1:27

Lord, I reject that lie that being Your follower is complicated or confusing. It's not. Your Word is clear: You value helping children and women who have lost those who were meant to provide for them. God, open my eyes to see who those people are around me. Whether it's an older neighbor who's lonely, a student in foster care, a widow at my church, or a child my family sponsors overseas, show me how to love others with Your love. Amen.

Think about it:

*What one person in your world
is God inviting you to help?*

DOING WHAT'S RIGHT WITHOUT ARGUING

Be glad you can do the things you should be doing.
Do all things without arguing and talking about
how you wish you did not have to do them. In that
way, you can prove yourselves to be without blame.
PHILIPPIANS 2:14–15

Father, I learn in Your Word that You not only want me to do what is right, but that You want me to do it with a pure and willing heart. And sometimes that's hard! It's difficult to do what I *should* do when what I'd really prefer is to do what I *want* to do. So help me to obey You and obey my parents without arguing or complaining. Change my heart so that I will be without blame, delighting in doing what is right. Amen.

Think about it:

In what area do you struggle to do what's
right that you can offer to God today?

GIVING THANKS ALL THE TIME

*Always give thanks for all things to God the
Father in the name of our Lord Jesus Christ.*
EPHESIANS 5:20

God, You are *good*! You are kind, generous, gracious, and merciful. Sometimes I fail to be grateful for who You are and all You have done for me. Forgive me. Today I choose to be grateful to You. Thank You for meeting my needs for food, clothes, and shelter. Thank You for providing caregivers for me and for all the people in my family. Thank You for the opportunity to learn, grow, and play. I give You thanks for so many things today in the name of Jesus. Amen.

Think about it:

*Is there a habit you can develop so that you
remember to give thanks to God? Can you
practice praying when your eyes first open in
the morning, or before you open your lunch at
school, or as your head hits the pillow at night?*

THEN YOUR LIGHT WILL SHINE

"Is it not a time to give clothes to the person you see who has no clothes, and a time not to hide yourself from your own family? Then your light will break out like the early morning, and you will soon be healed."
ISAIAH 58:7–8

Lord, I confess that a lot of my thoughts are about myself and what I want. Sometimes I forget about Your people in need. Forgive me. I know that You long to love others through me. God, make me Your servant today. Open my eyes to those in my home, at my school, in my community who have real physical needs: those without food, those without shelter, those who are sick. I know I'm limited, but show me how to do what I can do to care for the ones you love.

Think about it:

In the face of really big needs, what is one small thing you can do to help?

WHEN I'M WEARY

"Come to Me, all of you who work and have heavy loads. I will give you rest. Follow My teachings and learn from Me. I am gentle and do not have pride. You will have rest for your souls. For My way of carrying a load is easy and My load is not heavy."
MATTHEW 11:28–30

Sometimes I feel like I'm carrying a big, heavy load, and some days it feels too big for me. But I know that Jesus promises to help me shoulder my burden: my worries, my problems, my concerns, my fears. God, thank You for being a helper to me when I'm worn out. I know that I can curl up beside You, wrapped in my favorite blanket, and close my eyes and rest because You are with me. Thank You for being my good helper. Amen.

Think about it:

Where is a special quiet place that you can be alone with God as you let Him help you carry what's too heavy for you to hold alone?

GOD'S BIG LOVE FOR PEOPLE WHO SIN

"I tell you, there will be more joy in heaven because of one sinner who is sorry for his sins and turns from them, than for ninety-nine people right with God who do not have sins to be sorry for."
LUKE 15:7

Lord, You know that I try to be good, and because I work hard to be good, it's hard for me to see people who don't. I don't like it when I see people being unkind to others, or stealing things, or lying to their parents, or cheating in school. But Your Gospel reminds me that You really love people who sin. (Both me and others!) And You rejoice in heaven when one of these sinners turns to You. Father, help me to love sinners like You do and to help them know what Your love is like. Amen.

Think about it:

Is there someone you've written off as a "sinner" whom you can love in Jesus' name today?

KEEPING IN MIND WHAT GOD SAYS

*Look for the Lord and His strength. Look for
His face all the time. Remember the great
and powerful works that He has done. Keep
in mind what He has decided and told us.*

PSALM 105:4–5

Father, there are a lot of voices telling me who I should be. These loud voices tell me what I should buy, who I should imitate, how I should look, what I should watch, and how I should act. But I choose to ignore them, setting my eyes and ears on You. Lord, remind me of all You have done and what You have spoken in Your Word. Today I set my mind and heart on You. Amen.

Think about it:

*What is one way that you can keep God's words
in front of you today? (Write them on the front
of a school notebook? Scribble one word on
your lunch sack? Tell a good friend?)*

WHEN THINGS ARE HARD

We have this light from God in our human bodies.
This shows that the power is from God. It is not
from ourselves. We are pressed on every side,
but we still have room to move. We are often
in much trouble, but we never give up. People
make it hard for us, but we are not left alone.

2 CORINTHIANS 4:7–9

God, if I had my choice, I would always feel strong, sure, brave, and bold. But because life can be hard and following You can be hard, there are a lot of times when I feel challenged, weak, pressed, and hurt. But in Your upside-down way, You actually promise that when I'm most weak, You're strong! So shine through my cracked and broken places. Thank You for living in me and through me. Amen.

Think about it:

When have you seen God at work through you
because you were weak and not strong?

WHAT MY WORDS ARE SUPPOSED TO DO

Watch your talk! No bad words should be coming from your mouth. Say what is good. Your words should help others grow as Christians.

EPHESIANS 4:29

Not only do You invite me to grow strong in You, You also command me to help others grow as Christians too. And one of the ways I help others grow is through the words that I speak. I want to be someone who is faithful to honor You with my voice as I bless others. Father, let the words that pass through my lips today be ones that come from You. Help me speak words that are true. Help me find words that are good. Help me offer words that help others grow. To the glory of Your name, Amen.

Think about it:

Is there an area of speech where you struggle to honor God? How can you give that to God this week?

HELP ME TO SEE SIN

*A wise man sees sin and hides himself,
but the foolish go on, and are punished for it.*
PROVERBS 22:3

God, I believe that You have created me for abundant life, but when I sin, I reject the good life You offer. Forgive me. Today I need You to help me recognize sin. Show me the sins I've committed with my body. Point out the sins that are simmering in my heart. Shine a light on the sin in my mind. Spirit of God, like a doctor who checks out everything about me, show me where sin might be hiding in my life so that I can turn from it and toward You. Amen.

Think about it:

When has God shown you an area of sin in your life? Did you allow it to continue, or did you acknowledge the sin and turn from it?

THE SPECIAL INGREDIENT THAT HOLDS IT ALL TOGETHER

And to all these things, you must add love.
Love holds everything and everybody together
and makes all these good things perfect.
COLOSSIANS 3:14

God, I thank You that You have chosen me to be Yours and that I am loved by You. Through Your Word, You've shown me how to live well. And every day I do my best to obey You and to be Your faithful servant. In it all, You have commanded me to live with love. When I'm at home, when I'm at school, when I'm at church, when I'm with my friends, You promise that love is the special sauce that makes everything better. Today, help me to love with Your love. Amen.

Think about it:

Who is the most difficult person in your family for you to show love? How can you do it well today?

REMEMBERING MY SALVATION

Your loving-kindness toward me is great. And You have saved my soul from the bottom of the grave.
PSALM 86:13

Father, I confess that I get tangled up with the small things in life. I focus on little things—what I'm going to wear to school, who I'll sit with at lunch, or what I want for my birthday—and I can forget the really *big* thing: Your love! But I want to fix my heart and mind on what matters most. Today, help me remember that You have saved my soul. You have rescued me from death, and I belong to You. Help me to remember, moment by moment and hour by hour, Your loving-kindness toward me. Your steadfast, faithful love gives me life. Amen.

Think about it:

What is one way that you can hold on to the big truth today that God loves you?

LOVE GOD THROUGH LOVING PEOPLE

" 'When did we see You had no clothes and we gave You clothes? And when did we see You sick or in prison and we came to You?' Then the King will say, 'For sure, I tell you, because you did it to one of the least of My brothers, you have done it to Me.' "
MATTHEW 25:38–40

Lord, if I had the chance to care for You the way I'd care for a friend, I'd do it. You know I would. And Your Word says that I can! When I feed someone who's hungry, clothe someone in need, or visit someone who's lonely, it's really like I'm doing it for You. That's kind of amazing. And, if I'm honest, a little bit scary. Lord, give me the courage to love You by loving others. Open my eyes to those who have big needs, and show me how I can help. Amen.

Think about it:

Is there a way that your family cares for those who have really big unmet needs?

YOUR WORD GIVES ME EVERYTHING I NEED

All the Holy Writings are God-given and are made alive by Him. Man is helped when he is taught God's Word. It shows what is wrong. It changes the way of a man's life. It shows him how to be right with God. It gives the man who belongs to God everything he needs to work well for Him.
2 TIMOTHY 3:16–17

My Bible isn't just a heavy book with lots of words; it is how You talk to me! God, I thank You for speaking to me through Your holy and living Word. It's how You teach me. It's how You love me. It's how You help me. God, lift the words off every page and plant them in my heart so that I can become more like Jesus. Fill me with Your words and Your wisdom so that I can live as Your faithful servant. Amen.

Think about it:

Have you set aside a special time and place each day to read God's Word?

SCRIPTURE INDEX

OLD TESTAMENT

TRY THE DEVOTIONAL!

3-Minute Devotions for Girls

Written especially for girls, this devotional
packs a powerful dose of comfort,
encouragement, and inspiration into
just-right-sized readings for young hearts.
Each day's devotion is complemented
by a relevant scripture and prayer.

Paperback / 978-1-62836-638-9 / $4.99